Padre Pio of Pietrelcina

The Stigmata of Padre Pio
This exceptional photo was taken on 19 August 1919 by Padre Pio's
contemporary and classmate, Fr Placido of San Marco in Lamis. It is the first
known document of the stigmata, clearly visible, round and deep, on the back
of Padre Pio's hands.

Fr Francesco Napolitano

Padre Pio of Pietrelcina

a brief biography

✢✢✢✢✢✢✢✢

the columba press

EDIZIONI
PADRE PIO
DA PIETRELCINA

Published in 2015 by
ꞇhe columba press
55A Spruce Avenue,
Stillorgan Industrial Park,
Blackrock, Co. Dublin

in association with
Edizioni Padre Pio da Pietrelcina
Piazzale Santa Maria delle Grazie, 4
71013 San Giovanni Rotondo

Cover design by Helene Pertl
Origination by The Columba Press
Printed by ScandBook AB, Sweden

ISBN 978 1 78218 232 0

Originally published in 1978 as *Padre Pio: a brief biography*
by Edizioni 'Voce di Padre Pio'.

All photographs used courtesy of
Edizioni Padre Pio da Pietrelcina.

Contents

✝✝✝✝✝✝✝✝

Foreword

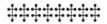

This is a book about the life of Padre Pio. It was written within five years of his death and was published in Italian and English before going out of print. Nearly forty years later, we have it made available in English once again.

Towards the end of the book, the writer, Francesco Napolitano, expresses the hope that the official request for the opening of Padre Pio's cause for canonisation in November 1969 would bear fruit.

In the intervening years, we have seen the cause for his beatification grow, and the demand that he be raised to the altars of the Church soon. The Prayer Groups that he set up following a request of his namesake Pope Pius XII to pray for an end to war, now marshalled their troops to ask God to see fit to make Pio a saint. And so it was that the Venerable Padre Pio of Pietrelcina was beatified in 1999 by another Pope, John Paul II, who then canonised St Pio of Pietrelcina in June 2002.

This book tells the story of a boy in Pietrelcina who never realised that the mystical experiences he had were not shared by others. This child was set apart by God for a special mission; one that the people of our time would be able to see and learn from. This is an account of a boy from rural Italy who was born Francesco Forgione, named after the country's patron saint, Francis of Assisi. Throughout his life, the boy who became Padre Pio was to bear a huge resemblance to the seraphic saint. He shared his name, his nationality, and later became a professed member of his Franciscan family. In his desire to suffer for souls and to be more like Christ, Pio of Pietrelcina was to bear the stigmata on his body, like Francis of Assisi.

This book takes us on a journey and shows how Padre Pio's mission was to suffer. Suffering was his hallmark and indeed, he deeply desired to suffer for Jesus Christ. From the moment he got up before dawn he counted the hours until he could offer the Holy Sacrifice of the Mass. He suffered until the moment he went to bed late in the evening.

He was ordained a priest in 1910 and it was soon after that he began to feel intense pain in his hands, feet and left side. It was as if the stigmata were announcing their presence in his life. In 1918, while deep in prayer in the choir at the foot of the cross, he began to bleed from his hands, his feet and his side. This caused him dreadful suffering, not only because the pain burned within him, but because he also knew that this would make him an object of people's curiosity. If only the stigmata would be invisible to people, he could hide a little better, but alas it was not to be. Only shortly before he died did the wounds begin to heal.

While he prayed for suffering, and daily offered himself in union with the sacrifice of the Mass, he always wanted to help heal others of their sufferings. This book gives many accounts of how Padre Pio spent countless hours at the service of ordinary people hearing confessions. In fact, such was the demand to go to Padre Pio for confession, that pilgrims from all over the world would need to queue in order to get a ticket to secure a time they could come and confess to him. While Padre Pio was very charitable and warm to most penitents, he was hard on people who came flippantly and those who weren't well-prepared to make a good confession. To some of the friars, he spoke about the price to be paid to gain back a soul for God; invariably, he himself was to pay that price far more than the penitent.

Perhaps the most famous account of Padre Pio's work in helping to alleviate suffering was the planning and construction of the Home for the Relief of Suffering. When Padre Pio asked his spiritual children to help raise the funds to build the hospital, people sent donations from all over Italy and the world, answering his call for help in this important project. This large modern hospital was his way of showing that his mission was to help heal people not just of their sins but also of their illnesses. Built a short distance from the friary where he lived all his life, today the Home for the Relief of Suffering is one of the largest and most modern hospitals in Italy.

There can be no doubt that Padre Pio dedicated his life to prayer and suffering. Every breath he took was a prayer – never for himself, always for others. From the beginning of his life he was able to easily travel from this world to the next, through deep prayer. He used this connection with

God to recommend to Him the prayers of his spiritual children. This ability to make contact with the powerful presence of God through prayer, enabled him to bless and pray with those in most need, wherever they were in the world. In the following chapters, we see examples of Padre Pio in prayer visiting South America, the United States, and parts of Europe. Those he visited would know that Padre Pio was present by the unmistakable aroma of violets and roses. Those who got closest to him noticed an odour of flowers emanating from the stigmata. To this day, forty-six years after his death, people will still insist that they have caught the scent of roses after praying for someone through the intercession of Padre Pio.

Padre Pio's priority was to be simply 'a friar who prays'. His intense prayer was offered up day and night for all his spiritual children and his religious community. He had a filial love for Our Blessed Lady, and spent much of his day praying the rosary. But Padre Pio was first and foremost a brother to the Capuchin Franciscan community of Our Lady of Graces Friary. Like the others, he daily lived the rule and life of the Order of Friars Minor. The first chapter of the Rule of St Francis outlines that the rule is simply to observe the Gospel of Jesus Christ living in obedience and in chastity, without property. As a Capuchin Franciscan, he promised obedience and reverence to the Pope, and to his superiors in the Capuchin Order. No doubt it pained him greatly when the cult of sanctity built up around him, causing difficulties for the Order with Church authorities.

Shortly before he died, the stigmata began to heal. When his body was examined by the doctors, they found that the wounds had healed and fresh white skin had grown. His life on earth was over, his earthly sufferings endured. He was journeying to the House of the Father where he prays for us all today in the presence of God.

Fr Bryan Shortall O.F.M.CAP.
Dublin, May 2015

Foreword to Original Edition

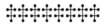

It is with profound joy and satisfaction that we acknowledge the publication, in English, of a brief and popular biography of Padre Pio.

By now, Padre Pio's fame has spread throughout the entire world. Even from behind the Iron Curtain, where news cannot infiltrate without being diligently examined, revised, and censored, we receive letters telling of the spiritual presence of this marvellous man; we hear of the prodigies obtained through his intercession.

In the plan of Divine Providence, Padre Pio was chosen in order to exercise his charisma and influence by awakening man's conscience to a sense of sin, to the reality of the supernatural. He was to call the wayward, the abandoned to the road of truth and grace; he was to kindle in everyone the vivid and everlasting memory of a suffering, crucified Christ, who died for love of man.

The newspapers of various nations have spoken both favourably and unfavourably about him.

Often, his greatness and magnitude were not rightly depicted, or else, were depicted capriciously, ignoring the supernatural quality of his special mission as a faithful servant of our Lord, ignoring his cooperation with Christ in the work of co-redemption and salvation.

Fortunately, educated people have written multi-lingual biographies which calmly and serenely reveal the precious moments of his life.

Since his death, the magazine, *The Voice of Padre Pio*, has regularly brought the various spiritual aspects of the Padre, as revealed by his writings, to the knowledge of his devotees. It has also presented the memories of those who had the fortune of either living near him, or of having at least met with him some time.

Every three months, the magazine, *The Voice of Padre Pio*, published in English, French, and German, unites in one spiritual family, all the devotees of Padre Pio who are scattered throughout the world.

Padre Pio has a very special characteristic: even from the silence of his grave he continues to exercise a marvellous influence. He seems to have a powerful magnetism, a fiery attraction, which interests people of all ages, all walks of life, all cultures. We, his fellow priests, the heirs and successors to his mission, testify to the vital, continuous miracle which can neither be denied nor concealed.

Although invisible, Padre Pio continues calling, reprimanding, comforting, and blessing all those who take the road to salvation; he continues to help all those who seek the grace of being cured in body and soul.

The author does not pretend to write a voluminous and critical biography; he simply wants to give his English-speaking brothers and sisters the opportunity of knowing

Padre Pio better, so that they may participate in the magnificent devotion of his admirers and spiritual children throughout the world.

We hope that this volume will not be the last, that it will inspire other English-speaking writers to make Padre Pio better known in the United States of America, in Britain, Ireland, Australia, Canada, the Philippines, and all those parts of the world where English is spoken.

We congratulate the author for his patient, accurate work and wish him the very best of luck.

> Fr Pietro Tartaglia
> Guardian of the Monastery,
> San Giovanni Rotondo, August 1977

Francesco Forgione

On 25 May 1887, at five p.m. in a small farming village, Pietrelcina, about twelve kilometres from the historic city of Benevento, Padre Pio was born. He was to some day amaze the world and attract its attention.

His parents, Grazio Mario 'Orazio' Forgione and Maria Giuseppa 'Beppa' Di Nunzio, born respectively on 18 October 1859, and 28 March 1859, lived in Vico Storto Valle, number 27 (today, number 32).

His father was a pure, modest peasant with a big heart and a strong faith. His mother was a virtuous woman who knew how to face the sacrifices of poverty with Christian courage; never guilty of recrimination or envy.

On the following day, 26 May 1887, their little son was baptised in the Church of St Mary of the Angels by the parish priest, Don Nicolantonio Orlando, and was given the name Francesco.

Francesco was given a Christian education, and was truly a model child. According to his mother, he was neither troublesome nor capricious, and was always obedient. Morning and evening he went to church to pay a visit to Jesus and the Madonna; he never had any desire to spend

Padre Pio's parents
His father was named Grazio Mario Forgione (1860–1946)
and his mother was called Maria Giuseppa Di Nunzio (1859–1929).

the day playing with his peers. Whenever his mother urged him to play with his companions, he refused to do so, because the children blasphemed.

'I have never played in my life,' Padre Pio was to confide regretfully, 'However, my father often tried.' Unlike his predecessor, St Francis, he had never been God's 'clown'. He had instead been a confessor of men, a witness to the evil, ugliness, and infinite misery of the world.

With a touch of melancholy in his voice, he would say to his friends and fellow priests, 'I was an insipid piece of macaroni, with neither salt nor sauce.'

Like an infant, he was unable to play because he didn't know how; he had discovered man too soon, and had suffered too soon for him.

From the following episode, little Francesco came to understand that believing in miracles was one way to combat ugliness in the world. 'He who believes in miracles has already obtained one.'

The event took place in 1896, the year that Francesco's mother found him sleeping outdoors on the ground one winter morning, with a stone for a pillow.

He had gone with his father to the feast of Blessed Pellegrino in Altavilla Irpina. The church was packed to capacity, and the smell of incense, garlic, and wine permeated the air. It was crowded and noisy: a typical religious feast of Southern Italy.

At one point, a raging, disheveled woman with bulging eyes pushed her way to the altar. She had a deformed child in her arms, her first-born. The unfortunate woman cried, screamed, begged and cursed; it was a heart-rending scene.

Little Francesco's father Orazio, being upset, wished to leave church in order not to see or hear any more. His son, on the other hand, persistently implored him to remain. Precisely at that moment, the distressed mother succeeded in reaching the main altar. Behold! Before the people who stood in silent awe, she prostrated herself on the steps, still holding the deformed baby. Then, suddenly, like an unchained fury, she stood up defiantly in front of the tabernacle, stretched out her arms, and presented the fruit of her womb. A chilling, single cry arose from the dumbfounded faithful; the woman was angrily throwing her child at the statue of Blessed Pellegrino, uttering these terrible words between sobs: 'Why don't you cure him? Keep him; he's yours!'

The child fell back into her lap. He was cured!

It was a true miracle. There was an indescribable crush as the people crowded hysterically around the feeble, human form that had just been cured. Orazio barely succeeded in saving his son from the human vice which was threatening to crush him.

Outside the church he gave Francesco a spanking. 'It's all your fault,' he scolded, 'all your fault.'

That peculiar son of his, who didn't know how to play, had ruined his feast!

The lodgings where Francesco was born and raised until the age of fifteen were placed in the custody of the Guardian of the Capuchin Friary, head of the Franciscan Seraphic Seminary for the education of future Capuchin priests. The friary and the seminary are located near the gate of Pietrelcina.

On the right-hand side of the road, in the garden facing the large building, there is a statue of St Francis of Assisi, and on the left, a monument in honour of Padre Pio. They seem to greet the arriving pilgrim and wish them *Pax et Bonum*.

Adjacent to the friary is the Church of the Holy Family which can be seen as somewhat reminiscent of the holiness of Padre Pio's family.

Francesco's childhood was characterised by his delicacy, his docility, and his profound religious devotion. At the tender age of five, he began entertaining the idea of consecrating himself to God. It was then that the first charismatic gifts appeared, along with the first assaults of the devil.

One of his spiritual directors, Fr Agostino of San Marco in Lamis, made the following testimony: 'The ecstasies and apparitions began at the age of five, when he first thought of consecrating himself to our Lord, and were continuous. When asked why he had hidden this fact for so long (since 1915), he candidly replied that he hadn't spoken of it, because he had thought it to be quite an ordinary thing that happened to everyone … The diabolical apparitions also began at the age of five.'

At the age of eleven, according to contemporary custom, he received his First Communion, and on 27 September 1899, with the utmost of spiritual joy, he received the Sacrament of Confirmation.

He received his first formal education from a private tutor, Domenico Tizzani, who, in addition to reading and writing, taught him a little Latin.

Tizzani was a former priest who had abandoned the habit in order to marry. For fear of judgement, he lived in Pietrelcina as a recluse, avoiding being seen in public; however, he tutored the children of the town for five lire a month. Francesco's tuition fee arrived directly from America, where Orazio had emigrated.

He taught his lesson regularly in a classroom that was always crowded. Francesco was among the most willing and the most disciplined of his students, even though Tizzani didn't consider him capable of continuing his studies.

Right from the start, Francesco began to take the blame for other children's faults.

Once, a student wrote an ingenuous love note to a classmate. The note, however, landed in the teacher's hands. In class, Don Domenico Tizzani insisted that the guilty person publicly confess to being the author of the 'sin'. From a bench in the rear, the guilty child stood up. He was not only guilty, but also a liar and a slanderer. To exonerate himself, he accused Francesco Forgione, who not only took the blame, but also the thrashing that was meant for the guilty party. Only after the punishment did it become known that he was innocent.

Many years later, someone reminded Padre Pio of the episode. 'It is clear,' someone observed, 'that you were predestined to be slandered.' And Padre Pio, with a half smile, replied, 'Poor teacher, how he regretted it later! ... But he wasn't able to take back the thrashing I received.'

The former priest's timid pupil not only learned how to

take the blame for others, but also how to share his gift of faith. In fact, his first convert, his first reconquered soul, was precisely that of the former priest.

Padre Pio recounted one morning he passed by his teacher's house. Don Domenico Tizzani was ill. In town, everyone said his condition was serious, but he, as usual, kept his personal life to himself. He had excluded himself from society by abandoning his sacred vestments. 'On the doorstep of the house,' Padre Pio recalled, 'there was an adolescent, his daughter. She was very upset. Her heartbreak and hopelessness shone in her tearful eyes, and she silently implored me as I passed. Her father was dying, abandoned by God and man … Ah, I couldn't resist, so I entered. The poor fellow's wife was there, ashamed and desperate like her daughter. What was I to do? … I told them to go to the kitchen, then I entered the bedroom … He died in my arms.'

He had reconciled him with God. That morning, long ago, he learned that in the world there are no reprobates or leprous sinners, only souls to be reconquered. Having become an apostle, Padre Pio became a most severe judge, but he also came to understand the sins committed because of love.

Padre Pio had four brothers and sisters: Michele, Felicita, Pellegrina, and Grazia. Before his birth, his sister Amalia died at the age of twenty-one months.

Speaking of his religious vocation, Fr Agostino of San Marco in Lamis tells us that something was developing in Francesco's innocent soul. Around the age of fifteen, he had

The youthful Padre Pio
This photo goes back to 1911, when Padre Pio was twenty-four years old.

an internal warning regarding the implacable battles he was to maintain with Satan. In fact, he had to deal with him when the time came for him to choose his vocation. The decision was enlightened by the gentle touch of grace.

Twenty years later, when writing to the teacher Nina Campanile of San Giovanni Rotondo, he recalled with emotion the personal battles he had sustained: 'Dear God! How can I describe the internal martyrdom that was developing in me? The mere memory of that internal battle developing within me makes my blood curdle, even though twenty years or so have passed. Dear God, I could hear the voice of duty telling me to obey You, but our enemies oppressed me, mocked me, dislocated my bones, and twisted my heart.'

On 6 January 1903, accompanied by his dear teacher, Angelo Caccavo, and the priest Don Nicola Caruso, Francesco was received into the novitiate of the Friars of the Capuchin Province of Foggia, in Morcone (Benevento). On 22 January, Francesco Forgione, dressed in the Capuchin habit, changed his baptismal name to Br Pio of Pietrelcina.

On 22 January 1904, kneeling at the foot of the main altar, surrounded by his dear mother, his brother Michele, his Uncle Angelantonio, and the entire religious family of the friary, he uttered his simple vows before the Guardian, Fr Francesco Maria of Sant'Elia a Pianisi, promising to live in obedience, poverty and chastity. At the end of the ceremony, Mamma Beppa, seeing her son was moved to tears, embraced him, kissed him, and said: 'My son, now you are truly a son of St Francis; may he bless you.'

Half a century later, in San Giovanni Rotondo, on 22 January 1953, remembering the emotion he experienced on that distant day, Padre Pio summed up his five decades as a friar, and wrote on the reverse side of a little holy picture: 'Fifty years of devouring fire for our Lord, for His redeemed. What more can my soul desire than to lead everyone to You, oh Lord, and patiently wait for this devouring flame to burn all my entrails *cupio dissolvi*, to be completely in You.'

On 27 January 1907, in the Friary of Sant'Elia a Pianisi (Campobasso), according to the canonical rule in effect at that time, he took his solemn vows '… with the sole and only purpose,' as he himself wrote on the official document, 'of attending to the good of my soul, and dedicating myself entirely to the service of God.'

Soon after the profession of his simple vows, Br Pio resumed the studies necessary for the priestly state: Rhetoric at Pianisi; Philosophy at San Marco la Catola and Sant'Elia a Pianisi; Theology at Serracapriola, Montefusco, and Gesualdo.

Among his teachers, who later became his spiritual directors, we find Fr Benedetto Nardella and Fr Agostino Daniele, both born in San Marco in Lamis of the Province of Foggia.

During the second year of Theology, on 19 December 1908, Br Pio received his minor orders at Benevento from the Archbishop Mgr Benedetto Bonazzi, and two days later, in the same city of Benevento, the order of subdeaconate from the Archbishop of Marcianopoli, Mgr Paolo Schinosi.

On 18 July 1909, in the church of the Friary of Morcone (Benevento), he was ordained a deacon by the Bishop of

Termopoli, Mgr Benedetto Maria della Camera. Finally, on 10 August 1910, in the Chapel of the Clerics in the Cathedral of Benevento, he was ordained a priest at the hands of the Archbishop Mgr Paolo Schinosi. His great hope became a reality; the joy of the Mass is difficult to describe.

On 14 August, he celebrated his first Solemn High Mass in Pietrelcina, and for the occasion, he wrote this thought: 'Oh, Jesus – my breath, my life – today, trembling, I raise You – in a mystery of love – may I be for the world with You – the Way, the Truth, the Life – and for You, may I be a holy priest – a perfect victim.'

His unstable health obliged him, before and after his ordination to the priesthood, to interrupt his regular course of study. The doctors and his superiors, hoping that a change of air would help him recuperate, sent him to his place of birth. Except for brief periods of interruption, he remained there until 17 February 1916, constantly battling against the mysterious ailment that tormented his fragile body.

For Padre Pio, this was a period of intense interior life and a persevering ascent on the difficult road of his spiritual journey. In fact, it was here in his paternal home that he received the invisible stigmata in the year 1910.

It is said that his mother, upon discovering him shaking out his hands, said jokingly, 'What's the matter, Francesco; are you playing the guitar?' 'Nothing, Mamma,' he replied, 'it's just that they sting so badly.'

It is a tremendous mystery that we cannot imagine, much less describe.

Jesus Christ wanted to try him, identify him with hidden, interior suffering, before putting him in the limelight to attract souls. Around the middle of October 1911, as stated in the biographical sketch at the beginning of the first volume of the *Epistolario* (a collection of Padre Pio's personal letters and correspondences, edited by Fr Melchiorre of Pobladura and Fr Alessandro of Ripabottoni), Padre Pio visited the famous doctor Antonio Cardarelli in Naples. Then, accompanied by the Minister Provincial, Fr Benedetto of San Marco in Lamis, he went to the Friary of Venafro (Campobasso) to take up residence in that community. But his illness became dangerously severe, and in order to avoid an imminent catastrophe, he was taken back to Pietrelcina on 7 December. The next day, to everyone's surprise, he celebrated Mass in the parish church as if nothing had happened.

No one could understand the cause of this mysterious illness. Padre Pio begged his spiritual director not to force him to talk, because it was God's will.

In the meantime, however, the Minister Provincial, Fr Benedetto, disapproved of him remaining at length with his family; this dissension caused him bitter suffering. But, since his illness made it impossible for him to return to the friary, Fr Benedetto obtained a decree from the Holy See on 5 March 1915, authorising Padre Pio to remain 'outside the friary for reasons of health, since this seemed to be the only means, the only hope of a cure'. He was to continue to wear the Capuchin habit, and remain under the obedience of the Minister Provincial.

Spiritual Director
One of Padre Pio's spiritual directors, Fr Benedetto Nardella (1872–1942).

World War I

When World War I broke out, even the Padre had to present himself to the military induction centre in Benevento on 6 November 1915, in order to fulfill his civic duties. On 6 December, he was assigned to the Tenth Medical Corps in Naples. However, by the eighteenth of the same month he was back home on medical leave, and remained there for one year.

On 18 December 1916 Padre Pio returned to military duty in Naples, and yet again, on the thirtieth of the same month, he received medical leave and was sent home.

On 19 August 1917 he was obliged to return to the barracks in Naples, and was unexpectedly declared fit for internal service. He remained at the barracks until the fifth of November, at which time he was once again written off on medical leave for four months.

He spent this period of time in the Friary of San Giovanni Rotondo, and on 5 March 1918 he resumed military service for the last time. However, ten days later, he wrote to Fr Benedetto and to Fr Agostino: 'I am extremely happy that divine grace has permitted me to be completely free of the militia.'

In fact, the day after writing these letters he was discharged following a serious lung ailment, with the declaration of good conduct on his discharge papers, and of having served his country 'with fidelity and honour' during the aggregate 182 days of military service.

We know very little about his service in the Holy Trinity Hospital in Naples. His contemporaries simply tell us that when Padre Pio put on his military uniform, he looked rather oppressed and awkward.

His military superiors, seeing his slackness and lack of competence, assigned him to the most thankless and least desired work. He was, according to Maria Winowska, an orderly, a dustman, a stopgap ... the laughing stock of everyone.

But it was not this that was painful to Padre Pio; it was the casual manner of the barracks, the foul language, the imprecations, the blasphemy of his roommates. This sad, deplorable aspect of military life caused him to suffer terribly.

But God had his own reasons which were, as usual, both disconcerting and beneficial. Called to help sinners, Padre Pio had to learn what sin was, not from books, but by seeing it up close, monstrously brazen, almost a challenge to Divine Justice. In the barracks, he not only learned about sin, but also learned to love the sinner. His eyes, purified by the grace of God, could look beyond the chains of sin, and see them truly as children of God.

In the testing fire, this contemplative slowly became seen for the apostle that he was. His army companions, especially the officers, seeing his docility, his extreme humility, and his concern for the wounded and the sick, began to like him. They even became more disposed to granting him a discharge, convinced that Private Forgione with his ill health, could no longer wear the military uniform.

What most impressed the doctors at the military hospital was his temperature, which almost always reached – or surpassed – forty-eight degrees Celsius.

Fr Damaso of Sant'Elia a Piansini, a contemporary of Padre Pio, wrote in his *Memories of Padre Pio*: 'When he was a soldier in Naples, he used to say to the nurses "Don't give me the thermometer, because it will burst and you will be the one to pay for it, not I." For this reason the doctors were obliged to use the bath thermometer to register his temperature.'

On 30 December 1916, he was sent home on 'an unlimited leave of absence', but his army records stated a leave of six months. At the end of six months, when Private Francesco Forgione failed to appear at roll call, he was declared a deserter. The sergeant of the Carabinieri of Pietrelcina received the order to find and return with an escort an individual named Francesco Forgione.

With papers in hand, the sergeant made the rounds of the neighbourhood, but no one was able to tell him where that soldier and deserter of the royal infantry lived. His investigation had come to nought. Sometime later, he communicated to the high command of Naples that, in spite of all his efforts, he was unable to find the slightest trace of Francesco Forgione.

Time passed. The sergeant thought himself to be rid of this unpleasant affair, when one fine day he received a new order: 'Intensify the search!' He made some uncomplimentary, tight-lipped mutterings in the direction of the superiors of Naples, and departed on a new search. This one would have been as unproductive as the first, if he hadn't stumbled upon Padre Pio's sister.

'Signora Felicita,' he said, extracting the paper from his pocket, 'do you by any chance know a certain person named Francesco Forgione?'

'Of course, I know him,' she replied, 'He's my brother.' 'What! Your brother! Would he then be Padre Pio?' exclaimed the poor sergeant completely bewildered. Naturally, he knew the young Capuchin well, but would never have made the link between him and this fugitive bandit he had been ordered to find.

Having been informed of his residence, he quickly wrote to the Carabinieri of San Giovanni Rotondo, asking for their sergeant to escort Francesco Forgione back to Naples as soon as possible. However, by a providential oversight, he neglected to mention the soldier's religious name. Thus, after two weeks, he received the reply that Francesco Forgione was unknown in San Giovanni Rotondo.

'What do you mean, unknown!' bellowed the sergeant of Pietrelcina. 'His own sister told me he was there!'

The new search and new interrogations were completely unproductive. In San Giovanni Rotondo, the Forgione family was unknown, and this 'Francesco' was a mystery.

The High Command of Naples became impatient. The

Carabinieri, who had been strongly reprimanded, were beating their brains, wondering what to do next. The deserter, Francesco Forgione, was nowhere to be found!

Finally, one fine day, the sergeant of San Giovanni Rotondo rang the bell of the Capuchin Friary, and confided his troubles to the porter.

'What! You are looking for Francesco Forgione? He is here with us! He is Padre Pio.'

The sergeant almost fainted. 'Padre Pio! Good grief!' Everyone in the village knew him and respected him. Padre Pio, a deserter!

Nevertheless, he could not hesitate. The order was clear.

When Padre Pio was informed, he got on a train immediately. As soon as he arrived in Naples, he went to the captain, who frowned severely: 'Private Forgione, do you know that you have been declared a deserter?'

Padre Pio wasn't the slightest bit perturbed. 'Oh, no, Captain! I am not a deserter. Here is my leave of absence permit. Read it. Leave of absence for six months, then await orders. I have obeyed; I have waited … The order reached me yesterday and I left immediately.'

The captain stared at him. The devil of a man was right! And to think that for two months so many poor fellows had been through so much trouble because of him, all thanks to an incompetent document … The case against him was closed.

'All right, all right!' muttered the captain, 'You may go!'

Thus Private Forgione extricated himself in a perfectly innocent manner. He had obeyed!

Putting aside his military uniform, Padre Pio went to San Marco la Catola around the middle of April 1918, to have a discussion with his spiritual director, Fr Benedetto, and resolve his doubts concerning the direction of his soul, doubts that tormented him. He was then sent to San Giovanni Rotondo, where he remained until his death fifty-two years later.

The Stigmata

The spiritual life of Padre Pio is based on Christ, and on the effort he made to be united with Him. It was his spiritual ascension, rather than the external facts recorded in the last chapter, that characterised his life during the years 1916–1922. The energetic activity of his heart was all focused on his absolute determination to know God, and to know the means by which he could be possessed by eternal Love.

'His young priestly heart,' said Felice Spaccucci, 'was perpetually tormented by his hunger and thirst to be always disposed to divine love. He yearned for spiritual unity by identifying his will with God's will; this yearning caused in him the symptoms of a real illness.'

Because of these feelings, his spirit became notably fortified, slowly climbing to the peak of perfection. His body became immersed in a flame of love, his soul filled with gentleness.

'I saw,' he wrote to his spiritual director, Fr Benedetto Nardella, on 24 January 1915, 'with the eyes of my spirit, rather than with the eyes of my body, someone thrust a sharp, flaming knife which pierced my heart and reached my entrails; he pulled it out with all his might, only to repeat the operation a short time later. These repeated blows filled my heart with a great love of God.'

'The pain and the joy which these inflicted wounds produce in me, are too vivid to be adequately described. But, my Father, both the pain and the joy are spiritual; my body has no part in it.'

In another letter sent to Fr Agostino Daniele, on 30 January 1915, he confirmed this force of love, and the state of immense joy which came with it: 'At one and the same time, my soul feels the atrocious martyrdom caused by the above mentioned flame and an extremely excessive joy; all of which fills my heart with a great love of God.

'My Father, I feel as if I were annihilated, with no place to hide from these gifts of the divine Master. I am sick, sick at heart. I can't take anymore. The thread is about to break at any moment, and I can hardly wait for that moment to arrive. My Father, how sad is the soul which God has infected with his love.'

Padre Pio, in his conviction that God is the epitome of being, of perfection, of hope, of power and goodness (wrote Spaccucci), found indescribable joy in contemplating His richness; this joy attracted God's perfection to himself. However, he always believed that his soul was not capable of completely possessing God, yet he had a profound faith in the Supreme Goodness.

Padre Pio's sensibility, made more pleasurable by the power and infinite benevolence of God, longed for the fusion of his heart with the heart of his Creator. At the same time, he maintained a constant battle with the infernal enemy. Padre Pio felt humanly unworthy to receive so many manifestations from God, and agonised over not being able to offer up a worthier soul. When God showered His bounty upon him, he was pained, incapable of fully appreciating such kindness.

'Father,' he wrote to Fr Benedetto Nardella, on 18 March, 'I am taking the liberty of confiding in you: I am crucified by love! It is too much for me!'

By now, Padre Pio was already on the high road to mysticism; so much so, that with every visit of his Beloved, his suffering and joy increased. In exchange for the ardent love that he had for God, he often received some manifestation.

In a letter dated 26 August 1912, he wrote to Fr Agostino Daniele: 'I was in church making my thanksgiving after Mass, when all of a sudden I felt my heart being wounded by a dart of flame, so vivid, I thought I would die. I lack the right words to make you understand the intensity of this flame; I am completely unable to express myself. Would you believe it? My soul, a victim of these consolations, becomes empty. It seemed as if an invisible force were setting my whole being on fire ... My God, what a fire! What joy! I have experienced many of these transports of love, and for some time I have felt as if I were out of this world. On other occasions, this fire was less intense; this time, however, in another instant, another second, my soul would have departed from my body ... it would have gone to Jesus. Oh! How wonderful to become a victim of love!'

In the biographical notes in the first volume of Padre Pio's *Epistolario*, it is written that on 30 May 1918, the Padre received the most important and substantial 'wounds of love'.

Between the 5th and 7th of August of the same year, the mystical phenomenon called 'transverberation of the heart' took place, a prelude, one might say, to the prodigious stigmata which occurred a month later on 20 September, and made a decisive change in his life.

Spiritual Director
One of Padre Pio's spiritual directors, Fr Agostino Daniele (1880–1963).

On the night of 5 August 1918, while Padre Pio was confessing the young seminarians, he was wounded by a being with a long flaming sword. Feeling the agony, he retired with difficulty, suffering from sharp pains that lasted for seven days.

Here is how he, himself, described this 'transverberation' to his spiritual director, Fr Benedetto of San Marco in Lamis, in a letter dated 21 August 1918: 'I was hearing the confessions of our boys on the evening of the 5th, when suddenly I was filled with extreme terror at the sight of a celestial being whom I saw with my mind's eye. He held a kind of weapon in his hand, similar to a steel sword with a sharp, flaming point. I saw the being, and saw him thrust the weapon into my soul in a split second. I was hardly able to cry out; I felt as if I were dying. I told the boy to leave, saying that I felt ill and didn't have the strength to continue.

'This martyrdom continued for seven days. What I suffered during this dark period is difficult to explain. Even my entrails were torn and strained by that weapon, and everything inside me burned. From that day on, I was wounded to death. In the depths of my soul, I feel an open wound which causes me to suffer assiduously.'

It is to be noted that Padre Pio was obliged to write everything to his two spiritual directors, Fr Benedetto Nardella and Fr Agostino Daniele, natives of San Marco in Lamis.

Here is how Padre Pio himself spoke of the last sign he received from his Love, Jesus Christ Crucified, on that painful and memorable day when the physical and spiritual pains caused by the stigmata manifested themselves. The stigmata became five in number, like those of Christ.

On 22 October 1918, he wrote to Fr Benedetto: 'What can I say in answer to your question regarding my crucifixion? Oh, God, what embarrassment and humiliation I suffer explaining what You have bestowed on this poor creature!

'Last month, on the morning of the 20th of September, in the choir, after having celebrated Mass, I yielded to a peacefulness, similar to a sweet sleep. All my internal and external senses, and even the very faculties of my soul, were indescribably serene.

'During this time, an absolute silence surrounded and invaded me; I was suddenly filled with great peace and abandonment, which effaced all else, including the turmoil.

'It all happened in a flash. And while this was taking place, I saw before me a mysterious Being, similar to the one I had seen on August 5th, differing only because His hands, feet, and side were dripping blood.

'The sight of Him frightened me; what I felt at that moment is indescribable. I thought I would die, and would have died if the Lord hadn't intervened and strengthened my heart, which was about to burst out of my chest.

'When the Being disappeared, I became aware that my hands, feet, and side were dripping with blood. Can you imagine this agony that I experienced, and continue to experience almost every day?

'The wound of my heart bleeds continuously, especially from Thursday evening until Saturday. Dear Father, I am in pain because of this wound, and because of the resulting embarrassment which I feel within my soul! I fear I shall bleed to death if the Lord does not listen to my heartfelt supplication to relieve me of this condition. Will Jesus, who is so good, grant me this grace? Will He at least relieve me of the embarrassment which these outward signs cause me?

'I shall raise my voice and shall not stop imploring Him until He mercifully takes away, not the wound, nor the pain which I ardently desire, but these outward signs which embarrass me, and which are indescribably and unbearably humiliating.

'The Being of whom I speak is none other than the one I mentioned in my letter of August 5th. He pursues His mission relentlessly, causing me extreme spiritual agony. I feel a continual internal rumbling resembling the gushing of blood.

'Dear God! Your punishment is just, and your judgement is right, but grant me your mercy Lord, with your prophet I shall always repeat Lord, do not punish me in your rage, or reprove me in the heat of anger …

'My Father, now that all my internal life is known to you, don't disdain to send me a word of comfort to alleviate all this harsh bitterness.

'I always pray for you, for poor Fr Agostino, and for everyone.

'Bless me, always, your most affectionate son, Brother Pio.'

That fateful day, 20 September 1918, was a Friday; the day on which Jesus was crucified.

The Minister Provincial was also Padre Pio's spiritual

director, and upon hearing of the event, he ordered the Guardian of the Friary, Fr Paolino of Casacalenda, to 'keep quiet and avoid publicity', and await his arrival in San Giovanni Rotondo.

But in spite of the rigorous and prudent reservation of the Superiors and of Padre Pio, the fact could not be hidden, and little by little, it became public knowledge.

It is well known how these prodigious events exercise an exorbitant influence on the faithful. First in the nearby towns – almost surreptitiously – then in the more distant towns, and later in the very distant towns. There was a great uproar, especially when the phenomenon reached the newspapers. Large crowds began pouring into the isolated Capuchin Friary. This gave rise to a multifaceted and efficacious priestly ministry.

The biographical section of the first volume of the *Epistolario* talks of how the stigmata not only aroused popular devotion, but also the curiosity of scientists; they especially claimed the attention of competent authorities.

Around the middle of May 1919, Dr Luigi Romanelli, head physician of the hospital in Barletta, arrived in San Giovanni Rotondo. He had been invited by the Minister Provincial, Fr Benedetto, to examine the extraordinary phenomenon from a scientific point of view. Two months later, on 26 July, Prof. Amico Bignami, head of the pathology department at the University of Rome, had his turn. At the request of the ecclesiastical authorities in Rome, he repeated the examination over the space of an entire week.

A third visit was made in this same year by Dr Giorgio

Festa, who was sent to San Giovanni Rotondo on 19 October by the Minister General of the Capuchin Friars. A fourth examination was made on 15 July 1920, by Dr Festa and Dr Romanelli.

Dr Giorgio Festa made this report in regard to his examination of Padre Pio: 'In the palm of Padre Pio's left hand almost corresponding to the middle of the third metacarpus, I discovered the existence of an anatomical lesion of the tissue, in a more or less circular form, with clean edges, having a diameter of approximately two centimetres. This lesion appeared then, as it now appears, to be covered by a reddish brown scab …

'The Minister Provincial, Fr Pietro of Ischitella, having visited Padre Pio shortly after the manifestation of the stigmata, had the clear impression that the wounds observed in the palm of either hand, internally penetrated the depth and corresponded with those which appeared on the back region … During my visit, in order to observe well the lesions of his feet, I helped him, myself, to remove his socks. They were considerably drenched with a bloody serum. On the back of both feet, precisely in correspondence to the second metacarpus, I perceived a reddish brown circular lesion, covered by a soft scab which looked exactly like the ones on his hands.

'On the anterior region of the left thorax, under the papilla, Padre Pio showed us another lesion in the form of an upside-down cross. It measured about seven centimetres in length … None of the surrounding tissues showed any trace of redness or edema. However, there was a more intense and more extensive hypersensitivity to pain in that area, than in the normal tissues surrounding the other lesions.'

At the age of thirty-one, Padre Pio had the Christian synthesis on his body, the signs of crucifixion, and from that moment was a living symbol of the Cross for more than fifty years.

It is obvious that the opinions and conclusions of the scientists and journalists could not agree on the origin and the nature of the stigmata. Nevertheless, the admiration and the veneration of the 'Stigmatised Priest of the Gargano' increased day by day.

In a letter written on 19 November 1919, the Secretary of State of His Holiness, Cardinal Pietro Gasparri, recommended some people to Padre Pio, and stated that he would 'be happy if you prayed for the Holy Father and me, because we are so needful of your prayers'.

On 22 March 1920, Mgr A. E. J. Kenealy, Archbishop of Simla, visited San Giovanni Rotondo; his visit had a profound effect on the English press. On 20 May of that same year, Mgr Bonaventura Cerretti (later Cardinal), Titular Archbishop of Cornith and secretary of extraordinary ecclesiastic affairs of the Vatican, did the same.

In July, the Procurator-General of the Passionists came in the name of Pope Benedict XV, together with the famous Roman doctor, Prof. Bastianelli. The Supreme Pontiff said at that time that 'Padre Pio was one of those extraordinary men whom God sends, from time to time, to convert men.' On 25 October 1921, there took place the visit of Cardinal

Augusto Silj, Prefect of the Supreme Tribunal of the Holy See and Apostolic Delegate of the Sanctuary of Pompeii, in the company of Mgr Giuseppe De Angelis, of the same pontifical delegation.

It is to be noted that Padre Pio had the singular signs of the crucifixion for half a century, and that all those who had faith in the stigmatised friar of the Gargano received, and are still receiving, so much assistance, and give testimony of their serenity and faith in life. Others, who, for whatever reason never knew him, are sad. They are sad because they realise that they did not, or could not, take advantage of the great gift that God made to humanity: to see, in the likeness of Padre Pio, the copy of His only begotten Son.

Yet there is the conviction of so many people that Padre Pio, by virtue of the suffering caused by the stigmata, has brought, and will bring, so many souls to Christ. He would never permit that any of them should suffer while he was still on earth. It is up to those who were close to him to give full testimony of his teaching, and above all, to be obedient to the Church.

This, and only this, can prove the validity of the lesson his pain has taught us. Once again these words will ring true: 'By their fruits you will know them.'

Finally, the most dazzling gem in the millennial history of the Church, is that Padre Pio was the first priest to bear the stigmata.

Padre Pio's Mass

Padre Pio's life on earth was in perpetual union with God; all of his letters give valid evidence of this.

In a letter written to his spiritual director, Fr Benedetto of San Marco in Lamis, on 8 September 1911, he expressed himself in this manner: 'My heart beats very fast whenever I am with Jesus in the Blessed Sacrament. It sometimes seems to me that it will leap out of my chest. Sometimes, at the altar, I feel as if my whole being were on fire; I cannot describe it to you. My face, especially, seems to want to go up in flames.'

In another letter to Fr Agostino of San Marco in Lamis, written on 12 March 1912, he wrote: 'I have a great desire in my heart to tell you so many things, all about Jesus; but I don't know how to express myself, and my eyesight is failing.

'Yesterday, on the feast of St Joseph, only God knows how much happiness I experienced, especially after Mass, so much that I still feel it within me. My head and my heart were burning, but it was a fire that was beneficial to me. My mouth felt all the sweetness of the immaculate flesh of the Son of God. Oh! If only at this moment, while I am still feeling it, I could succeed in burying this consolation in my heart, I would certainly be in paradise!

'How happy I am with Jesus! How gentle is His spirit! But I become confused, and can only cry and repeat: Jesus, my nourishment! What afflicts me most is the fact that so much love from Jesus is repaid with ingratitude.

'He always loves me and always holds me close to Him. He has forgotten my sins, and possibly recalls only His mercy ... He enters me every morning, and pours into my poor heart all the effusion of His goodness ... This Jesus almost always asks me for love. And my heart, rather than my lips, replies: Oh, my Jesus, I want ... and then I can't continue. But finally I exclaim: Yes, Jesus, I love You; at this moment I believe that I love You, and feel the need to love You more; but, Jesus, I have no more love in my heart. You know that I gave it all to You; if you want more love, take my heart and fill it with Your love, and then order me to love You; I shall not refuse. As a matter of fact, I beg You to do it; I desire it.'

Here is a simple example of how a soul in love with God feels; there is no need to ask why. Padre Pio was the faithful friend of Jesus; his meeting with his Divine Friend took place every morning at dawn, at the altar; the meeting was visible to everyone who attended his Mass.

For such occasions he thought it necessary to prepare himself for several hours, in order to be worthy. In order to celebrate Holy Mass at dawn, and spend several hours in spiritual preparation before Mass, he would spend the night meditating on the great miracles which, through his priestly powers, would soon be in his wounded hands.

The friars who were close to him can testify to the hours he spent in pious recollection, while they themselves were struggling to stay awake.

The desire to have Christ in his hands was always agonising, and only the sight of the altar would placate him.

He never failed to cry when he celebrated the Divine Sacrifice.

The thousands of pilgrims who came to San Giovanni Rotondo during the fifty years of Padre Pio's priestly life, and had the privilege of participating in one of his Masses in the Sanctuary of Santa Maria delle Grazie, were witnesses to the uniqueness of the celebration.

'A Mass that I shall never forget,' wrote C. Cree. 'I attended many of Padre Pio's Masses,' wrote Maria Winowska, 'but no two were alike. Certainly the Padre was rigorously faithful to the rubric, and his manner was marvellously sober; nevertheless, it was clear that he was not alone in the process. Some sort of presence surrounded, seconded, and hindered him. One Friday I saw him breathless and oppressed, brusquely shaking his head, struggling in vain to get rid of an obstacle which was preventing him from pronouncing the words of the consecration. It was like a hand to hand battle in which he was the victor, but which exhausted him. At other times, from the 'Sanctus' on, large drops of sweat ran down his forehead wetting his face which was tearfully contracted.'

On Mount Gargano, which was sanctified by his presence, Padre Pio renewed the Sacrifice of Golgotha every morning at five o'clock; there he offered himself as a victim, a sacrifice for poor sinners.

As soon as the doors of the church opened, around four o'clock, there was a terrible commotion to get to the altar where the Padre was to celebrate Mass; everyone wanted to be as close as possible. Then, as soon as Padre Pio could be seen in the doorway of the sacristy, a veil of silence, of divine mystery, immediately fell upon the faithful, creating an air of profound meditation, a heavenly sensation.

As a rule, his Mass lasted about an hour, but no one tired of attending, nor was anyone bored or distracted. It was the best time to amend one's own faults before God.

The greatness of Padre Pio's Mass lay in the knowledge that Jesus Christ performed His works through the wounded hands of a man.

After reading what took place on the altar, one might suppose that Padre Pio was selfishly wrapped up in his celestial joy, but in reality he was always close to his spiritual children, making their worries and sorrows his own.

One day, a woman whose husband was ill, came to San Giovanni Rotondo asking that he be cured through the intercession of the celebrated stigmatist. All through the Mass she did nothing but change seats, eager to be first in line to place her petition. Every attempt was in vain, so the poor woman rejected the idea of giving Padre Pio her petition as he passed, in favour of seeing him in the confessional. Holding onto this ray of hope, she entered the sacristy, only to find it very crowded. Reluctantly, she wondered if it was time to give up.

All at once Padre Pio appeared in the doorway, and all the women rushed forward to be able to kiss his wounded hand. Making his way through the crowd, the Padre approached the poor, tearful woman, and in a voice that was half joking, half severe, he said to her, 'My dear, when will you stop moving about from left to right, constantly buzzing in my ear … Do you think I'm deaf? You have already asked me five times. I have understood. Go home and everything will be all right.'

We can therefore hazard to say that although Padre Pio appeared to be 'heavenly self-centred', he never failed to notice those who needed his assistance, even when they were at a distance.

Padre Pio celebrant
Padre Pio's prayers reached the most sublime heights of mysticism during the celebration of Holy Mass.

Padre Pio had a great influence on priests who came to San Giovanni Rotondo and attended his Mass; many of them recaptured their fervour through the merits of Padre Pio, and are today saintly priests and great apostles.

One such priest wrote to the magazine *Epoca* on 20 September 1968: 'I am a priest who, years ago, went to Padre Pio in the company of a man who was seeking a cure. I was delighted to have the opportunity of studying the mystery of the Friar … I shall say immediately that I wasn't able to prove anything.

'The sick man whom I accompanied was not cured; I smelled no perfume, nor did I have any visions. Moreover, when I went to confession, Padre Pio did not lift any mysterious veil from my soul. For me, he was nothing more than a good confessor, very much like all the others, I would say … and yet, there was something unusual.

'For many days I attended Padre Pio's Mass, and for me, it was everything. I listened to the Mass from the upper balcony, at the side of the altar, missing neither a gesture nor an expression.

'I had already celebrated thousands of Masses, but in those moments, I must confess, I felt like a poor specimen of a priest, because Padre Pio truly spoke with God during every moment of the Mass; I should say that like Abraham, he struggled with God. God was present in his Mass, and not just in the Eucharist, as in my Mass.

'Thus, in San Giovanni Rotondo I found a priest who truly and intensively loved God, in suffering and in prayer, loved him to the point of agony. A true saint!

'I don't know whether Padre Pio has ever performed any miracles; I only know that such a man could perform hundreds of them.'

Another priest, Fr Domenico Mondrone, a Jesuit, wrote in the magazine *La Civiltà Cattolica*: 'Anyone who has ever attended Padre Pio's famous Mass, will never forget it; one had the vivid impression of seeing time and distance, between the altar and Calvary, annihilated.

'When the Divine Host was raised by those hands, the mystical union between the offering priest and the Eternal Priest, was rendered more sensitive to the eyes of the faithful. At the sight of this, even the curiosity-seekers were profoundly touched.'

It can be said that the celebration of Padre Pio's Mass literally upset the course of his, and everyone else's existence. It had polarised the attention of the world; it had even regulated the bus schedule, and the schedules of the hotels. Everyone was practically convinced that Padre Pio's Mass was such an exceptional event that it could not be repeated.

That is why Nino Salvaneschi, an Italian writer, wrote this marvellous page on Padre Pio's Mass in his book *Breviary of Happiness*: 'Never has any man of Christ manifested greater simplicity in his imitation of Christ praying in Galilee. His face pale, his eyes half closed, as if he were seeing a sharp ray or light, Padre Pio said his Mass at that simple and almost coarse altar, in an atmosphere that transcended this life; he seemed to belong to a humanity that was superior to ours. Gathered around him were the crowds of San Giovanni Rotondo who sounded like the murmuring sea, agitated by the south-west wind.

'Waves of people push forward to the altar, up to the three steps where, many times, various bishops knelt to serve Mass. And the crowd encircled the altar of the mystical Mass, like an immense rosary of suffering humanity ... And this was the Mass that Padre Pio said for the people of Puglie, a region scorched by the sun and battered by the Adriatic wind; it was also the Mass that he said for the crowds that came from distant places, from the cities of Europe, from America ... Certainly that man was truly with God when he celebrated Mass.'

At Padre Pio's Mass, there are those who cry, those who suffer, those who pray rapturously, and those who, by means of an unforeseen divine light, come to know their sins and visibly repent. The early morning vigil causes no fatigue; worldly things are forgotten. Time flies because everyone is united to the celebrant. With Christ crucified, they offer, they love, they adore.

Meanwhile, as Padre Pio retires, everyone's knees seem to be nailed to the floor.

In the early years, Padre Pio began his Mass at noon, immediately after hearing the women's confessions. Later, because of a prohibition for a period of time, he was obliged to celebrate Mass in the private chapel of the friary. And there it seemed even two hours were insufficient for his Mass. In his later years, he always celebrated Mass at five o'clock in the morning.

Three years before Padre Pio's death, the chronicles of the friary made the following notation: 'On 20 September 1965,

Padre Pio got up about one o'clock in the morning, made his preparation for Mass, went down into the sacristy about ten minutes to four ... When the time arrives that he can celebrate Holy Mass, he can no longer endure it. The thought of the Mass is a constant disturbance; sometimes when he wakes up during the night, he asks the time, or whether it is time to celebrate Mass. Even during an illness, when, for a few days he was unable to go downstairs to celebrate Mass, he wanted to receive Holy Communion as quickly as possible, even before four a.m. He became calm only after receiving Communion.'

On 29 March 1911, Padre Pio wrote to Fr Benedetto: 'I have such a hunger and thirst to receive Jesus, I could die of anxiety. Because I cannot bear not to be united with Him, I am often obliged to receive His Flesh when I have a fever.'

This ardent desire, born of faith, which sustained and confirmed him, benefited those for whom he obtained graces, especially his spiritual children, and all the pilgrims who came to see him.

On the altar of Santa Maria delle Grazie, the pilgrims saw the miracle of living faith, since Padre Pio 'impelled by free-will and grace, firmly substantiated the revealed truth.'

His Priestly Ministry

Padre Pio, in his religious and priestly life, was always the simple friar, the simple priest. He never had any special assignment in the Order, except for having been the director of the Seraphic Seminary in San Giovanni Rotondo during World War I.

He had no special academic titles other than those required of anyone who aspires to the priesthood. He was gifted, however, with a quick and ready mind, a prodigious memory, a tremendous goodness, and a profound doctrine. He had the gift of communicating peace to all those who sought his help. He sympathised with the miserable, consoled the afflicted, and eased the pain of the sorrowful. His priestly paternity, his sympathy and tolerance, led him to love his fellow creatures as if they were his children, or his brothers and sisters. He was the people's servant, everyone's friend and the sinner's brother.

His brotherhood was not focused on sin, but rather in redeeming the sinner. He stood lovingly beside anyone who confessed their faults, and followed them closely until their salvation was assured.

He was the good shepherd who found no peace until the straying sheep were brought back to the fold. Like Moses, he was a most worthy leader, directing souls towards perfection, towards Paradise and the Promised Land. For this goal, he employed every spiritual means to keep his penitents from straying to the false path of apparent virtue.

His confessional was neither an institution of education, nor a tribunal pronouncing a sentence; it was, instead, a clinic for souls. In the confessional he fulfilled his paternal mission forcefully, tenderly, patiently, courageously, compassionately, and correctively; according to individual needs, and for the good of the penitent soul.

He was both mother and father for his spiritual children; a father because of his strong, unlimited courage; a mother because of his tenderness. He would fan the flames of their Christian duty by threatening and correcting them, before lovingly consoling them in the various afflictions of their lives.

He was not a lenient confessor; on the contrary, he was most severe – never irresolute, never accommodating. Everyone trembled before him. With his scrutinising eyes searching for the most secret wounds of the soul, nothing could be hidden from him; he upset even the shrewdest of people. Although his words were sometimes brief, they still had to penetrate the secret of the soul – to shake it up and root it out – to renew the person. He used sugar-coated words only when there was profound pain in the soul of the penitent. He never compromised with evil, no matter who the sinner was. Although his inflexibility and severity could be drastic, they are a testament to Padre Pio's concept of sin, and the pain it caused him. 'I don't give candy to someone who needs a purgative.'

He was as harsh with superficial, insincere, hypocritical penitents, as he was kind and affable towards those who were sincere and firmly resolute.

Very often he was brusque, and uttered harsh, emphatic words, such as when he sternly reprimanded women, especially, for scandal, lies and gossip. Not to mention sins against purity, against maternity, blasphemy, and violation of the religious days of obligation; he would not absolve these sins unless he found the necessary disposition in the penitent. It was not rare for him to shut the door in the face of the penitent before interrogating them, even those who received Communion frequently elsewhere.

God would often permit him to see, in a flash, that which was hidden from other confessors.

In the confessional, Padre Pio had his own method, his own style, an absolutely personal and charismatic art; the result was that he penetrated every heart and led everyone to God.

Cardinal Giacomo Lercaro said of Padre Pio, the confessor: 'He was firm and decisive to the point or being brusque and almost rude, but at the same time, he was so open and comforting that he gave peace and serenity to those who lacked it for years, or perhaps had never had it.'

All in all, Padre Pio's confessional was extraordinarily crowded every day – a near unmanageable crowd gathered around his confessional in double file.

For fifty-two years, from 1916 to 1968, he was 'the confessor', 'the apostle of the confessional', and 'the martyr of the confessional', from morning till night.

For Padre Pio, the confessional and the altar were his whole life.

The town of San Giovanni Rotondo, hidden in the Gargano mountains, was unknown to everyone. From 1918, that bitter and impressive solitude, that rocky desert, began to come to life and bloom. The Gargano, in short, was transformed into a 'holy mountain', and the entire credit goes to that stigmatised priest enclosed in the confessional.

When Pope Paul VI received the Minister General of the Order on 20 February 1971, it was not by chance that he had this to say of Padre Pio: 'See how famous he became! People from all over the world gathered around him! But, why? Perhaps because he was a philosopher? Because he was a scholar? Because he was wealthy? Because he celebrated Mass with humility! He heard confessions from morning until night, and was, though difficult to believe, a man bearing the imprint of the stigmata of our Lord.'

Burning with love of God on the altar, Padre Pio made the confessional incandescent. 'I love souls', he often said, 'the way I love God.'

From these few notations our readers have become acquainted with the Padre's spirit, his reason for spending so much time in the confessional. His heart burned with the desire to redeem souls, and at the same time, alleviate their physical sufferings. That was the reason it was so difficult to restrain the crowds that flocked to his confessional daily.

On 7 January 1950, in order to discipline the enormous crowds that came from all over the world, and to re-establish order in the church, the Superiors deemed it wise

The Dispenser of God's pardon
Padre Pio spent the greater part of his day
administering the Sacrament of Penance.

to establish an Office of Reservations. This ensured that every pilgrim would have the possibility of seeing Padre Pio in the confessional.

If we go back to his early years as a priest, we will see how much Padre Pio suffered because of this distinct vocation for the confessional. His vocation was opposed. It seems incredible, yet that's what happened. Mystery in the lives of the saints!

In the *Epistolario* of Padre Pio, we find eighteen letters which were written in the space of two years (April 1911 – April 1913). These letters contain Padre Pio's pressing requests to the Minister Provincial, who was also his spiritual director, to grant him the faculty of hearing confessions; they also contain Fr Benedetto's decided refusal, for various reasons, to grant him this faculty.

In answer to Padre Pio's urging requests, and in answer to Fr Agostino who intervened, pleading his cause with the Fr Provincial, the following reasons were given by Fr Benedetto for his refusal: '… because, my son, I expect that it will be extremely harmful to your health, and perhaps, even to your peace of mind'. Several days later, Padre Pio received another letter from the Minister Provincial: 'I cannot grant you the requested faculty, not only because I am concerned about your health, but because I must also be certain of the necessary qualifications before authorising anyone to the sacred ministry.'

In the face of this refusal, Padre Pio accepted the will of Heaven, and anxiously waited. A year passed. Then, one day, knowing that his dear Fr Agostino was going to San

Marco la Catola to meet with the Minister Provincial, he wrote the following: 'Dearest Father, when you go to San Marco la Catola, I beg you to pay my respects to the Minister Provincial. I also hope you will ask him once more, to authorise me to hear confessions. I am sure of failing, but I can no longer suppress this mysterious voice within me. I am disposed to the will of the Guardian, so that one additional refusal will only mean greater resignation on my part.'

Finally, the desired day arrived! On 12 May 1914, the Padre wrote to Fr Agostino describing the pastoral visit of the Archbishop of Benevento to the parish of Pietrelcina, and added: 'You will understand how we have all been extremely occupied with the confessions and instruction of the older children in order to dispose them to the Sacrament of Confirmation.'

From these words we can see that if the Padre was numbered among the confessors, surely, he must have already been granted the faculty of hearing confessions.

Unfortunately, however, those who are truly called by God to undertake heroic missions, must at first clash with seemingly insurmountable human obstacles. And indeed, this is what happened in Padre Pio's case.

Fr Benedetto's severe judgement regarding the confessional was the fruit of human prudence, presuming to be better than the judgement of the Holy Spirit. However, the Spirit worked mysteriously and productively in Padre Pio, his soul was dedicated and open to grace.

His love for his brothers, and the mysterious, unsuppressible voice in his heart, were the personal reasons why

Padre Pio was persistent in asking the Minister Provincial to authorise his hearing confessions.

It is a shining example, in line with true Franciscan tradition, that Padre Pio gives to the Capuchins of today, and to all priests of our times: he inspires them to lovingly dedicate themselves, even to the point of heroism, if necessary, to the ministry of the confessional, the most fruitful of pastoral duties.

A few years previous, Padre Pio wrote to Fr Agostino: 'If you don't hear from me often, please don't blame me; it is not because I'm unwilling to write. I've told you everything, besides, you ought to know that I never have a free moment. A multitude of souls thirsting for Jesus pounce on my back; it's enough to make me pull out my hair! Faced by such an abundant harvest ... I am made happy by the Lord, because I see the ranks of chosen souls increasing constantly; Jesus is loved more and more.'

This multitude of souls never left him a free moment. Cardinal Corrado Ursi of Naples made these remarks: 'Padre Pio was, for the entire span of his life ... nailed to the confessional. The portentous ministry of the confessional was more characteristic of him than were prayer, penance and prodigies. The people who came here from every part of the world, generally did not ask for graces and miracles; they wanted him to hear their confessions. Only for this reason did they face the discomfort of a long journey, and often a long sojourn in San Giovanni Rotondo; they wanted to await their turn in the confessional. And yet, Padre Pio's confessions were neither easy nor accommodating; they weren't compassionate caresses that minimise everything.

On the contrary, they were uncomfortable and difficult for anyone who lacked sincerity, who was not truly penitent, or who refused to change his way of living. In that confessional of his, God's mercy existed only for those who accepted the light, agreed to the penalty for their sins, and were willing to die in order to be re-born.'

The confessions of other priests were not substantially different from Padre Pio's; the difference lay in the great number of conversions, which Cardinal Ursi confirms: 'He possessed a special charisma for this ministry, by means of which he easily penetrated the conscience in order to stimulate it, to help it respond, to improve, to humbly accuse itself, to be sincerely penitent, to hope for deliverance. He directed the penitents – often refusing absolution in such a brusque manner, it would break even the most hardened hearts – to die and be re-born, to change their lives. There were many such interesting cases.'

Volumes and volumes could be written about the many interesting conversions which took place in San Giovanni Rotondo; we will cite only a few.

One of them is the conversion of Ferruccio Caponetti, a militant, materialistic mason. He described his conversion in a letter written on 18 November 1931: 'I climbed the rough path of Mount Gargano and found the master who greeted me with joy because he realised that I was blind. With a smile, he listened to all my doubts; then, with a profundity of thought, uttered with the simplest of words, he demolished, one by one, all the theories in my mind. I was unable to oppose any of his arguments. He laid bare my soul, showed me the sublime teachings of our Lord, and reopened the eyes of my spirit. He reached my heart and I saw the light; I knew the true faith. Now I know the true God, and feel a tremendous peace in my soul … I owe all this to Padre Pio.'

'These few words so full of emotion (wrote Winowska), marvellously determine the decision regarding the non believer's drama. Padre Pio does not make all the difficulties disappear by uttering a few supernatural words. He helps the rebel intellect understand by reading his conscience, by being wonderfully patient and courteous, by removing the mental block. Would he have had so much success in intellectual circles if he had acted otherwise?'

Another noteworthy and interesting conversion concerns a young man who was planning to murder his wife and make it look like suicide, in order to freely throw himself into an illicit relationship. To avoid suspicion, he had consented to accompany his wife to Padre Pio. No sooner had he set foot in the church than he felt himself attracted to the sacristy, as if by a magnetic force. At that moment, Padre Pio was hearing the men's confessions, and when his turn arrived, the young man knelt down too. The Padre looked at him severely with those scrutinising, penetrating eyes, grabbed him by the arm, shoved him forcibly, and shouted: 'Get out of here! Get out of here! … You shameless creature, your hands stink of blood, yet you have the temerity to go to confession!'

The man ran, terrorised. His soul was so jolted, such a terrible storm arose in him, that he had no peace for two days. For three nights he didn't sleep; terrible visions upset him. On the third day, early in the morning, he was among the first waiting behind the church door to hear Padre Pio's Mass, during which, he did nothing but cry. Even he had been renewed by Padre Pio, in love and in pain. He returned to the sacristy, and when Padre Pio saw him kneeling to make his confession, he welcomed him as Jesus had welcomed the great sinners. With a sweet, serene smile, he placed his wounded hands on the young man's head, comforted him, and exhorted him to persevere in living a good life.

Fr Tarcisio tells us that one day, when they were climbing the steps of the friary, after hearing confessions, a man approached Padre Pio saying that he wished to make his confession. The Padre stared at him; then with a severe look and unyielding tone, his face darkening, he said: 'Don't you see how black your soul is? Go, put your affairs in order, change your way of living; then come back, and I will hear your confession!'

The scene upset Fr Tarcisio. After a few steps he said, 'Padre, doesn't it make you uneasy?' 'My son,' replied Padre Pio serenely, 'only the external has assumed a different appearance. I have not changed internally. And since I do not wish to displease my brother, I'll have you know that it pierced my heart like an arrow! But if I didn't do that, so many would not convert to God.'

The stigmatised priest of the Gargano used to say: 'If you only knew what a soul costs; souls are not given as a gift; they are bought. You don't know what they cost Jesus. Now we still have to pay for them with the same coin.'

He frequently made these gentle, paternal admonitions to his spiritual children and to his penitents: 'My son, how you have made me suffer! ... How you have made me labour! ... Your soul has cost me so much! ... I paid with my blood for your soul!'

Padre Pio's entire priestly life was contained between two most brilliant lights: the altar and the confessional. There was no better place for anyone to meet the Stigmatist of the Gargano.

Padre Pio was either on the altar, immolating himself before Jesus and our Heavenly Father; or he was in the confessional, proclaiming the message of Divine mercy and forgiveness – a sort of permanent Good Friday.

The Sacrifice of Calvary, the Sacrament of Divine Mercy and heavenly pardon, are the visible components of Padre Pio's fruitful priestly mission.

End of a Spiritual Direction

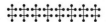

Towards the middle of 1921, it was rumoured that Padre Pio would probably be transferred.

Since the Vatican exercised extreme prudence, the transfer was made known only to the Superiors of that time. Even so, the news spread rapidly to the four corners of the town, causing an uprising against the priests, the Archbishop of Manfredonia, the friars, and even against Padre Pio himself, as we shall see.

The populace was disposed to even sanguinary action, preferring to see Padre Pio dead in San Giovanni Rotondo rather than alive elsewhere.

The crowds were exasperated, but he who paid the price was Padre Pio, naturally.

One of the key participants in the events of those turbulent years, was the Mayor of San Giovanni Rotondo, Francesco Morcaldi, who recounts: 'One morning, when Mass was over, there came forward from among a group of young people who crowded the rectory of the small church, a man with a revolver. Pointing the revolver at Padre Pio's back, he shouted that he would keep him there dead, rather than be abandoned by him. The frightened, screaming crowd barely had time to disarm him.

'He was undoubtedly excessively rash, and aroused to brutality by the passion of the rabble who had a long battle to wage against an unknown factor, in order to retain their famous "Paragon of Virtue".'

On the other hand, the daily newspapers – which were not always accurate – added to the influx of crowds that became increasingly uncontrollable. Even though the majority of the visitors were devout, composed, and sincerely religious, there were many fanatic, imprudent frauds.

In order to avoid abuse, and to alleviate the situation existing in the Friary of San Giovanni, the Holy Office intervened. On 2 June 1922, some directives were sent to the Minister General of the Order, who in turn transmitted them to the Guardian of the Friary, ordering that Padre Pio be kept under observation, and to ensure he was neither singled out nor lost in the clamorous crowds. He was not to celebrate Mass at a regular time, but rather, at various times of the day, preferably early in the morning, and in private. He was not to give his blessing to the people, and 'under no circumstances was he to show the so-called stigmata, nor speak of them, nor allow anyone to kiss them'.

A few months later, the news of Padre Pio's imminent transfer reached San Giovanni Rotondo; the people were incensed.

On 16 October 1922, the mayor sent the Guardian a petition consisting of about fifty pages of signatures, and the following protest:

'We, the undersigned citizens of San Giovanni Rotondo, having been informed of the removal of Padre Pio of Pietrelcina from the Capuchin Friary, do protest against such measures, and advise the ecclesiastical authorities of the Capuchin Order that should the attempted transfer be effected, we will impede his removal with every means at our disposal, including extreme measures. We will engage in reprisals against anyone who is believed to be responsible for the removal of this Friar who has made our town illustrious, who has radiated so much good in this suffering world, and who has earned the devotion of these citizens. – San Giovanni Rotondo, 27 September 1922.'

After the signatures of the citizens of San Giovanni Rotondo, the Mayor added: 'I hereby disclaim any responsibility for the regrettable consequences and inevitable public disturbances which the above-mentioned measure will cause; the responsibility will fall entirely on the authority that chooses to disregard the justifiable protest of this population.'

In May 1923, the local Guardian, Fr Ignazio of Jelsi, was unofficially advised that our Padre Pio would be subjected to more severe restrictions and prohibitions; on 31 May, a communique was received, and the following notation was made in the friary chronicle: 'The Guardian is awaiting orders from the Minister Provincial.' The latter replied, 'Orders will arrive.'

The orders arrived punctually. The Minister Provincial tried to prepare everyone by writing to Padre Pio: 'Be prepared to drink the bitter chalice that I have just drunk.'

Padre Pio remained as calm as he had when faced with other communications of that sort. All he said was, 'They won't keep us waiting long. They will soon tell us what we are to do.'

On 17 June 1923, the Guardian received the orders, 'cut and dried'. They were almost the same as those of 2 June 1922: 'that Padre Pio was no longer to celebrate Mass in public, but was to celebrate Mass in the private chapel of the friary with no one in attendance; that Padre Pio was not to answer letters which he received from devout persons seeking his counsel, prayers, etc. – nor was anyone else to answer these letters for him.'

Fr Ignazio of Jelsi adhered to the orders and made Padre Pio celebrate his Mass privately, but it wasn't long before he was obliged to write to the Minister Provincial, Pietro da Ischitella, in the following terms: 'When the people noticed that Padre Pio was no longer celebrating Mass in the church, they maintained that the rule was an offense, almost a punishment inflicted on him. They became convinced that more severe rules would follow the first, so they formed a committee, met in the square, and decided to do their utmost to obtain the revocation of that rule. The Mayor, on behalf of the people, sent telegrams of protest to both ecclesiastical and civil authorities.'

On 25 June 1923, a crowd of about three thousand people, accompanied by music and by civil and military authorities, went straight to the friary demanding that Padre Pio not be transferred, and that he be permitted to celebrate Mass in public.

The following day, Padre Pio celebrated Mass in the church again; however, it wasn't long before another order arrived from Rome, on 22 August 1923. It declared that Padre Pio was to be transferred to Ancona, to the Minister

Provincial of that province, and was to be subject to the Minister General.

The Provincial of the Marches, Fr Cherubino of Castelnuovo, felt that the city of Ancona 'was not a place suitable for saints', and decided to allocate his 'precious gift' to the Friary of Cingoli.

On 4 August 1923, the Provincial wrote to Fr Pietro of Monte Roberto, who was then the Guardian of the Friary of Cingoli: 'In that remote Friary [Padre Pio] could live in peace and be of help to the friars [confessors].' He ended his letter with a question: 'The Friary of San Giovanni Rotondo is surrounded – night and day – by devotees who are interested in seeing that Padre Pio is not removed. Will those friars succeed in transferring him?'

History tells us that the Minister Provincial's question was answered negatively. And many years later, reminiscing about those troublesome days, Fr Ignazio of Jelsi told the friars: 'As soon as it was decided to transfer Padre Pio to the Capuchin Province of the Marches, a priest, whose name I don't recall, came from Ancona; I don't recall precisely whether he was the Guardian of the Friary of Cingoli. We were talking about how to get Padre Pio out of the Friary of San Giovanni Rotondo without provoking any incidents, when the Capuchin of the Marches proposed this strategy: We were to prepare, in the garden of the friary, a wagon containing two barrels, one full of wine and the other empty, so that we could put Padre Pio in it and quickly leave for Foggia! ... It was a proposition that I could not accept, because I simply could not fill a barrel with Padre Pio; and because the consequences would later have fallen completely on my shoulders.'

But while so many people were concerned about Padre Pio, he himself was not perturbed; he continued to live his life placidly, obediently complying with the slightest order. He never made any observations, no matter what changes took place in his life; however, in spite of his serenity, he was not made of stone; even Padre Pio was a man who could suffer.

Fr Alessandro of Ripabottoni wrote, in his book on Padre Pio: 'He observed all that was happening to him and for him, and bit by bit, painfully but generously united his own will to the will of Christ crucified under obedience.'

Meanwhile, time passed and the waters became more turbulent and agitated; Fr Luigi of Avellino, Provincial Vicar, went to the Prefect of Foggia, not only to inform him of the orders of the Superiors, but also to ask whether the intervention of the Government would be necessary.

The Prefect, Mr. Mormino, replied: 'The orders will be executed even if we have to trample on dead bodies.'

Sometime during the first two weeks of August 1923, Fr Luigi showed Padre Pio his transfer orders; the latter bowed his head, folded his arms, and replied: 'I am at your disposition. Let's leave immediately; when I am with the Guardian, I am with God.'

In the meantime, an envoy of the Chief of Police, Carmelo Camilleri, arrived from Rome to settle the case and to take the necessary precautions. In his report to General Emilio De Bono, Chief of Police, Camilleri declared: 'a show of force with inevitable bloodshed would have been necessary' to remove Padre Pio from the Friary of San Giovanni Rotondo.

General De Bono was so impressed by his official's report, the circumstances, and the assembled evidence, that he became the promoter of the revocation of the transfer orders, by means of authoritative emissaries.

While it appeared that the town and the friary were finally at peace after so many months of upheaval, the one who suffered most was our own Padre Pio.

Soon after this sorry affair, Fr Luigi of Avellino, Foggia's Vicar Provincial, was removed and sent to the Friary of Frascati (Rome) to act as Guardian.

Shortly before that, on 2 June 1922, Fr Benedetto was ordered to abstain from speaking and writing about Padre Pio, and from maintaining any correspondence with him.

Rome deemed it opportune that Padre Pio have a spiritual director other than Fr Benedetto. Thus, Padre Pio was deprived of his truly great spiritual teacher, and was never again to see him in this life.

Padre Pio suffered immensely because of this deprivation! But he accepted his suffering in utter silence and in complete submission to the divine plan.

And so, the spiritual direction of Fr Benedetto Nardella of San Marco in Lamis came to an end.

The Man of Suffering

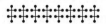

To speak of suffering in regard to Padre Pio may seem superfluous, considering the fact that he was the personification or pain, and hence, the man of suffering. Indeed, he was the man of suffering because he was acquainted with pain in all its moral and physical aspects, because he knew how to imitate the first Person who suffered for love. He became a perfect replica of Him.

Padre Pio's suffering was not of the common variety. It was not suffering due to the limitations of life and death, to a lack of energy and intelligence, to poverty, or a terminal illness; it was a suffering that was permeated with radiant joy, because by means of it, he could lead souls to Christ.

It was essentially a beatitude for Padre Pio, as his letters to his spiritual directors and spiritual children reveal, since it permitted him the knowledge and possession of Christ in an absolute sense. This constituted his energetic force.

One day, after some early and intensive apostolate work, the friars who took care of Padre Pio, convinced him to go to bed and rest. The Padre consented to their persistent advice, but soon after said he wished to get up again. His fellow priests, surprised by his request, said: 'But, Spiritual

Father, you wish to get up so soon?' and Padre Pio retorted: 'How can I remain in bed with all the frightening things that God makes me see?'

On another occasion, when the strain on his physical health was pointed out to him, he replied: 'If you only knew the worth of a soul.'

Natural suffering necessarily requires rest; supernatural suffering, although rest is willfully neglected, will multiply one's strength for the glory of God, a glory which will someday delight the spirit of the suffering person.

From childhood, Padre Pio had the special grace of understanding that life is pain, so he transformed it by exalting pain. He said to a spiritual son, in the confessional, 'My son, life is primarily suffering and pain; we must love and appreciate it, especially because our Lord has given it to us.'

On another occasion he said: 'We must embrace the cross which Jesus gives us; it is our salvation, our strength and our comfort during our short pilgrimage on earth. Pain brings us closer to Jesus.'

'Suffering,' he often repeated, 'is the most beautiful thing for a Christian.'

'One doesn't get to Heaven by car, money cannot buy souls; the kingdom of Heaven is reached by the road of prayer and suffering.'

Padre Pio lived solely for Christ. He hid himself in the mystery of Calvary and spent the fifty years of his priesthood in perpetual crucifixion, in a generous silence based on charity and humility. He was a perfect imitation of St Francis, the Poverello of Assisi; having learned from the latter how to make a perpetual offering of himself, he was chosen by Providence for the colossal work of charity which was to benefit his brothers in pain.

For Padre Pio, suffering was a true vocation, because he never refused to save souls; the pain that he offered for the salvation of souls likened him to Christ.

He conquered souls by means of his own passion, by shedding his own blood from his wounds, and by spending his nights in fruitful vigil. 'I shall pray for you,' he said to a spiritual daughter, 'even when you make me suffer; I want your salvation, because I have become a victim for you.'

In this son of the Poverello of Assisi, pain became a force of attraction; everyone who knew him realised that he was an enlightened man, sustained by the grace of God. Even atheists, Masons, sovereigns, princes, intellectuals, theatre and movie stars, kneeled and bowed their heads in the presence of that mask of pain; they knew that humble friar was not just interpreting the drama of the passion, but was its true protagonist, especially when he celebrated the Divine Sacrifice of the Mass.

Even the common man, in the presence of that suffering friar, would wonder about the problem of pain, and to his silent question – 'Why do you suffer?' – Padre Pio would answer silently: 'Because in our present circumstances, suffering, alone, can prove our love for God.'

In the confessional, he would often say to the souls who understood it, 'Onward, for love of Christ. Onward, still a little more suffering.'

In keeping with this attitude, in keeping with the Christian vision which he inculcated in the hearts of his most beloved children, all those souls who were able to comprehend the concept of Christianity through pain, can still affirm: 'I am not to be pitied; I am happy in my suffering.'

No one was ever able to explain Padre Pio's sufferings and illnesses during his lifetime. Doctors and fellow priests were constantly running to his bedside, but no one ever succeeded in alleviating his physical pains, nor was any doctor able to make a diagnosis.

During his agonising contortions he would say to those who were helping him: 'Do not worry; leave me alone; you cannot understand … it will soon be over.' And in fact, he'd be up and around again – sometimes in a matter of hours, sometimes in a few days – going about his business as if nothing had ever happened.

This is the way it was throughout his entire life. Not once did he complain about his pains; he was elated by his suffering.

In December 1948, Padre Pio was in bed with a high temperature, and exceedingly intense pains throughout his entire body. The doctors could not understand the cause. Fr Francesco Napolitano of San Marco in Lamis, who was at his bedside in the capacity of a nurse, hearing him lament repeatedly, 'Dear God, dear Mother, give me strength,' and seeing that alarmingly high temperature, said to him: 'Padre, why don't you let me apply a cold compress to your forehead?' He replied, 'My son, there is nothing you can do to help me; you are unable to understand.' However, when the priest insisted, he acquiesced saying. 'Do what you please.' As soon as the cold compress touched the forehead, the Padre exclaimed: 'Oh, how refreshing; God bless you, my son.'

On the third day, Padre Pio resumed his work as if he had never been ill. His life was full of similar incidents. Fr Agostino recorded many of these ups and downs in his diary.

In 1958, from 22 to 26 January, Padre Pio suffered with kidney stones. On the 22nd, he was unable to celebrate Mass, while on the other days he celebrated Mass, but was unable to hear confessions.

One morning, Fr Francesco Napolitano was on duty to make reservations for confessions, and to attend to Padre Pio. Shortly after four a.m., he left the private chapel of the friary where he had just celebrated Holy Mass, and started down the dimly lit corridor to offer his services to Padre Pio. There he saw the outline of a person who was bent over, dragging himself along by holding on to the wall for support. He realised immediately that it was Padre Pio, and ran to help him.

In answer to the priest who gently reproached him for leaving his room too soon, and without assistance, he said: 'My son, I feel so bad; I can't take it anymore; however, let me go to the sacristy for Mass.' Then, leaning on Fr Francesco's shoulder, he dragged himself to the sacristy to continue his preparations for the five o'clock Mass.

In his later years, Padre Pio had many relapses; he was

worn out, extremely weak, and exhausted from pain.

In the manuscript *The Debility of Padre Pio*, Fr Rosario of Aliminusa tells us: 'He always seemed to be at the extreme limits of his strength, and perpetually at the point of death. When he said goodnight, Padre Pio always added, "I commend myself to the Lord, because I don't know whether I will see tomorrow's dawn." He had no fear of death, but always felt that it was close at hand ready to snatch him at any moment … His fatigue was most intense at sunset.'

Due to his illness and the burden of his years, he walked with extreme difficulty. It was 29 March 1968 that the Superiors convinced him to use a wheelchair, and this was what he did until his death.

He was a man who knew physical weakness and pain right from the first years of his life in Pietrelcina. His sensibility – as a man, as a priest, as a Franciscan – made him determined to deal with the problem realistically. To eliminate pain is impossible; to relieve it is possible; so he did this, as a moral duty. This was the starting point of Padre Pio's suffering.

His mission to help other people was expedited by many offerings which the good people placed in the wounded hands of the Padre, to be used for the benefit of the needy.

In January 1925, with the closing of the former convent of the Sisters of St Clare, the doors opened to gather in the sick and the needy.

It was now the little 'Civic Hospital of St Francis', complete with two small wards, two little private rooms, with a capacity of twenty beds, and sanitary equipment.

Padre Pio wanted to get involved in this project. The heartbreaking condition of the sick demanded it of him; the generosity of the faithful, and the collaboration, courage, and tenacity of Dr Leandro Giuva and his committee, enabled him to realise it.

However, the life of this hospital, which was born of love, was brief – only thirteen years. It was left to deteriorate after it was seriously damaged in the earthquake of 1938.

Yet the St Francis Hospital was merely a rough copy of the more immense project that was to follow. For many years Padre Pio had nursed a dream that was to become a reality. On the night of 9 January 1940, in the little cell of Padre Pio, the 'Home for the Relief of Suffering' was born.

Three friends were with Padre Pio, 'three spiritual sons, three shipwrecked persons who had come to the serene banks of Faith, from very different shores': Dr Guglielmo Sanguinetti, the municipal doctor of Ronta in Borgo San Lorenzo (Florence); Dr Carlo Kiswarday, a pharmacist from Zara, Yugoslavia; Dr Mario Sanvico, a veterinarian from Perugia.

Padre Pio had spoken at length about his mission, and his words, in spite of their serene simplicity, were an ardent elegy on the afflictions of humanity. 'In every sick person, there is Christ who is suffering! In every poor person, there is Christ who is languishing! In every sick person who is poor, Christ is doubly there!'

This is how the idea of the hospital was born; it was born and became immediately operative. The Padre, after searching the pockets of his tunic, pulled out a small gold coin which had been given to him by an anonymous little old lady, for his works of charity. Holding it up, he said, 'I want to make the first donation for the Home for the Relief of Suffering. Tonight, my great project begins. I bless you and all those who will help my work! It will always grow in beauty and size.'

Padre Pio's great institution had its beginnings at that time, and since then, there has been an influx of contributions, large and small.

Providence Opens Hearts

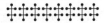

The Home for the Relief of Suffering was already legally established. Having drawn up the legal documents for the establishment and ratification of the hospital, Padre Pio was anxious to begin the work, no matter the cost. The numerous issues were carefully studied, and on 6 May 1947, the work was begun with the placing of the first stone. By 19 May 1947, explosives were blasting the barren mountain to make room for the foundation of one of the most remarkable monuments to brotherly love, where every stone, every object, every installation is an expression of love from one brother to another.

The work began and progressed without any particular financial plan; the money arrived from various and unexpected quarters, but always from the same source: love and charity. Some people offered ten or twenty lire; others offered a million, but for those in charge of the work the twenty lire were worth as much as the million.

Providence opened the hearts and the hands of man, so that he could sustain the work and alleviate his neighbour's suffering.

One day, Miss Barbara Ward, editor of *The Economist*, who was in London with the Marquis Patrizio, expressed the desire to meet 'the famous Padre Pio' she had heard so much about.

'Go to Foggia,' said the Marquis, 'I will accompany you.'

They took the plane to Rome, and then continued on to San Giovanni Rotondo. Upon approaching the friary, Barbara was amazed to see a priest in charge of twenty labourers who were working on the road. She asked him what he was doing, and the priest, Don Giuseppe Orlando of Pietrelcina, replied: 'We are building a large hospital.' 'How much will it cost?' she asked. The priest dropped a bomb when he replied. 'Four hundred million.' 'Who's paying for it?' 'Whoever passes by, pays.'

The lady passed by, and went to see the Padre.

'Everyone in London speaks so highly of you that I have come to ask you a favour.' 'Yes, my dear, our Lord grants favours.' 'Father, I am a Catholic, but my fiancé is Protestant; I should like him to convert to Catholicism.' 'Yes, if God so desires, he will be converted.' 'But Padre, when?' 'If it is God's will, it could happen right now.'

The English lady returned to London, not quite satisfied with the Padre's answer. But to her amazement, she found that her fiancé had been baptised a Catholic on the very day, at the very hour, that she had spoken to Padre Pio. She told her fiancé of the miracle, and begged him to go quickly to Padre Pio to thank him, adding: 'Bear in mind that they are building a hospital, and are in need of four hundred million lire.'

Her fiancé, who was the managing director of the United Nations Relief and Rehabilitation Administration (UNRRA), came not only to kiss the wounded hands of Padre Pio, but also to make him a proposition.

'Father,' he said, 'I know that you need money; well, then, if you will consent to naming this hospital in honour of Fiorello La Guardia, I can help you.'

Fiorello La Guardia, a native of Foggia, had been the Mayor of New York and director general of the UNRRA. Padre Pio shrugged his shoulders and heartily agreed.

A few days later, Barbara's fiancé, Mr Robert Jackson, went to America to inform Fiorello La Guardia's widow that a large hospital was being constructed in Italy to honour the memory of her late husband, and that he had obtained the sum of four hundred million lire from the UNRRA and was sending it to San Giovanni Rotondo. The widow quickly sent a telegram thanking the Italian Prime Minister, Alcide De Gasperi. The latter, who knew nothing about the project, referred the matter to the Prefect of Foggia, who in turn phoned the Provincial Medical Officer expressing his amazement that a hospital was being built in San Giovanni Rotondo, without the permission of superior authority. The provincial physician, also in the dark, hurried to San Giovanni Rotondo accompanied by members of the Prefecture and the Police Department. But once they came face to face with Padre Pio, they all calmed down, and the provincial physician was happy to inform Padre Pio about the four hundred million lire. He also promised to give his complete support, and advised him to quickly send the plans for the hospital to be approved by the Department of Health in Rome.

This was only the beginning; it took six months of battling to obtain the money from Rome. The money finally arrived, but not all of it. One hundred and fifty million lire was deducted from the original four hundred million, and allocated to other charitable institutions.

Hearts became generous in regard to the work that was to be accomplished; a chain of friends and spiritual children of the Padre collaborated untiringly to obtain the necessary assistance. Money 'flowed like an inexhaustible river' from all parts of the world. Rich and poor, Italians and foreigners, all gave wholeheartedly, some more, some less. They all answered the Biblical maxim: 'He who gives to the poor, gives to God.'

The work was difficult but productive. Padre Pio's presence and approbation were a most welcome and most efficacious encouragement to all those who had dedicated themselves to this holy work. In November 1952, he personally supervised the progress by visiting everything – from the offices of the management, to the terrace for the helicopter-ambulance.

To a group of eminent surgeons and technicians who met on 8 May 1955, to resolve the organisational problems and discuss future activities of the hospital, Prof. Di Raimondi of the University of Bari said: 'It is a work which has its origin in a religion based on charity for the suffering. It is an intensive study of clinical and biological facts, a study enlightened by faith. It is a work that stems from the will and sacrifices of an occasional rich person, a few prosperous people, and an amazingly large number of poor people from all over the world. It all took place under the silent but incessant influence of the prayers and good example of a Franciscan Friar, Padre Pio, who withdrew in order to engage in a transcendent dialogue with the Eternal Father, but came forward unselfishly, and unsparingly, to accomplish the mission of consoling souls.'

Finally, the news that everyone was anticipating, arrived. On 5 May 1956, the feast of St Pius, the inauguration of the Home for the Relief of Suffering took place.

Among those present were the Minister of State Braschi; Cesare Merzagora, President of the Senate of the Republic; Cardinal Giacomo Lercaro; the Minister General of the Capuchins, Fr Benigno of Sant'Ilario Milan; and internationally famous medical authorities such as Prof. C. Lian of Paris; Dr Lequime of Brussels; Dr Taquini of Buenos Aires; Dr P.D. White from the United States; Dr W. Evans from England; Dr G. Nylin of Sweden; Dr Mahaim of Lausanne; Dr Di Raimondi of Bari; Dr Condorelli; Dr Dogliotti; and so many others. There were also many bishops, innumerable priests, and about fifteen thousand people, not only from Italy, but from all over the world.

At the inauguration, Padre Pio said: 'I thank our benefactors from all over the world, for their cooperation. This is the product which Providence, assisted by all of you, has created. I present it to you. Admire it, and then, let us all bless the Lord, our God.'

'May the Lord bless all those who have worked: are working, and will work for this House; may He reward you and your families a thousand times over in this life, and grant you eternal happiness in the next.'

'It is useless to talk', said Cardinal Lercaro, 'when things speak for themselves in such an eloquent manner … There is a clear and precise way of finding God, and we have so much need of Him. There are moments in everyone's life when the need becomes acute; it is when our pride is overcome by suffering and humiliation that we finally look for God. Where can we find Him? The way is clear: Where there is charity, there is love; where there is love, there is God … Have you noticed this in San Giovanni Rotondo? Yes. The whole world has become aware of it. God is here; therefore, love and charity are also here.'

Home for the Relief of Suffering
The hospital Padre Pio built on the bare Gargano Mountain for the
relief and comfort of his neighbours' souls and bodies.

Prof. Paul Dudley White of Boston, President Eisenhower's illustrious doctor, said that the hospital was beautiful, perhaps even too beautiful. Impressed by the basic principles of Padre Pio's work, he transmitted his admiration to America: 'This hospital, more than any other in the world, in my opinion, is the most suitable for the study of the relationship between the soul and sickness.'

Pope Pius XII defined the Home for the Relief of Suffering as 'the fruit of a lofty instinct, of an ideal which was developed and perfected at length, and which is in touch with the most varied and most cruel aspects of the moral and physical sufferings of humanity'.

Finally, Prof. O. H. Wangensteen from the United States had this to say of the Home: 'Everything here is good and marvellous. I have but one regret: that there is only one Padre Pio in the world. It's a pity that there aren't more like him.'

One of the hospital's first activities was an international convention for coronary and arterial ailments. The most prominent personnel of the medical field attended and dedicated themselves to the study of the human heart, under the supervision of the illustrious consultant of the hospital, Prof. Pietro Valdoni.

Three days later, these doctors had an audience with Pope Pius XII, who said to them: 'The circumstances which motivate your presence here are a cause of great joy for us, and the beginning of a great hope for all those who suffer. In fact, to make the inauguration of the hospital of San Giovanni Rotondo exceptionally splendid, you have held a symposium on coronary ailments … It should be noted that the hard work, the preoccupation, the difficulty that invaded the progress of this project, did not succeed in lessening the enthusiasm that inspired it. From 1947 until 1956 it progressed with tenacious patience, and is now a magnificent success. It is one of the best equipped hospitals in Italy, a product of modern technology, and one of the best in Southern Italy … Now we can truthfully speak of an efficacious relief of suffering.'

At first the hospital was equipped with three hundred beds; today there are more than one thousand.

In 1957 there was a definite sign of the Pontiff's good will towards the Padre. On the 4th of April of that year, Pope Pius XII made Padre Pio the administrator of the hospital. It was a most amazing event, particularly since it has so rarely happened in the history of the Holy See.

Other constructions followed: the new Church of Santa Maria delle Grazie, with its bright centre and spacious aisles; the maternity school; the school for female nurses; the school for male nurses; and the Franciscan Confraternity House. They all add an evangelical touch to the Home for the Relief of Suffering.

There are also two flourishing periodicals printed in four languages: *La Casa Sollievo della Sofferenza*, and *The Voice of Padre Pio*.

Prodigies are endless in that 'land of souls'. The faithful increase in number everywhere, and are of the same mould, even those on the other side of the Alps. They are soon attracted by the call of a good and solid friendship. They unite in prayer groups, and hand in hand, subdue their interior anxiety by following the paths that lead to Heaven.

On the 10th anniversary of the Home, Padre Pio looked at all the good that had been accomplished, and all the good that was yet to be accomplished, and said to his spiritual children, friends, and benefactors: 'My dear children of Italy, and of the entire world, to all of you, near and far, may the peace and blessings of our Lord be with you.

'It is with a heart full of emotion that I speak to you on this memorable and solemn occasion. The work of Divine Providence during the past ten years has surely been prodigious and greatly beneficial to the Home for the Relief of Suffering.

'My blessed children, I thank you with all my heart for your generous gift, for your sacrifices, and for your interest and thoughtfulness. You have been the instruments in God's hands, for the realisation of this Home. Here the bodies and souls of our sick brothers are cured with the help of the priestly, medical, spiritual, and social facilities of the hospital.

'As a token of my gratitude and appreciation, I offer my prayers and suffering for all of you.'

Pastoral Joys

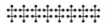

Every day of Padre Pio's life in the Friary of San Giovanni Rotondo was fruitful, because every day there was some prodigy, sent by Divine Grace, for the benefit of his children. It was precisely because of these prodigies that the Padre and his children drew closer and closer, and became united in a spiritual embrace.

For Padre Pio, the creation of a new life by means of Grace filled his heart with so much love, that he would have felt incomplete without it.

Padre Pio's love flowed like an immense river; that is why his heart was always prepared to grant love in the form of forgiveness, advice, and help.

Padre Pio's love for his children touched the soul, and was therefore invisible and immaterial; but from its inconceivable beauty were born true apostles who were paragons of Christian virtue.

The graces which he obtained were always for the benefit of his apostolate. When he cured the ailing body, his goal was the soul. He collected his best trophies in the confessional. Because he accepted the role of father, Padre Pio felt obliged to accept the spiritual responsibility of numerous souls; when a sinner reacted to his counsel and began to live in Christ again, his joy abounded.

Padre Pio realised that he had lit the torch of eternal life, so he kept it burning by his perpetual counseling and exhortations about living life to the full.

We might say that Padre Pio had two important rules: love of one's neighbour, and love of sacrifice. Love of neighbour was most important to him since he had offered his own life for humanity, especially for sinners; love of suffering was naturally closely linked to it.

From his native town, on 29 November 1910, Padre Pio wrote to his Spiritual Director, Fr Benedetto of San Marco in Lamis: 'For some time I have felt the need to offer myself to the Lord, as a victim for sinners, and for the souls in Purgatory. This desire has grown so strong in my heart that it has now become, you might say, a strong passion. It is true that I have made this offer to our Lord many times, asking Him to give me the punishments that were meant for sinners and for the souls in Purgatory; I have even asked Him to increase the punishment a hundredfold as long as sinners could be converted and saved, and the souls in Purgatory could enter Paradise sooner. I should now like to make this offer to our Lord with your permission. It seems to me that Jesus really wants it.'

By loving his children, the pilgrims, and all those who approached him, Padre Pio united himself more intimately with God. Those who were rehabilitated by Padre Pio's union with Eternal Love could not be amorphous creatures; they had to be dynamic. Padre Pio's spiritual children could be distinguished from other Catholics by their spirit of altruism, by their disposition to righteousness, by their public and private prayers, by their sacrifices which were known only to God, by their professional honesty, by their serenity and wholesome joy.

He wanted his children to smile, to show everyone that Christianity is joy and happiness, and that there is no need for faces to be darkened by frustration.

He once said to a young student, 'My son, smile; be happy even though your studies are not what you want them to be; while you're studying, relax, and enjoy yourself.'

Padre Pio's recurring advice to his spiritual children was to be good; to fear God, not because of His justice, but because of His love: 'Be good, my son, always fear God and live in His love. Blessed is he who loves the Lord and serves Him faithfully. I bless you.'

Very often among these souls there were those who came to San Giovanni Rotondo out of curiosity, or to poke fun at the poor friar that everyone was talking about. However, these people soon became the true heralds of Christianity, regenerated on the Gargano.

A certain visitor, who had come to San Giovanni Rotondo out of curiosity, was trying to hide behind a group of men who were gathered in the sacristy. Padre Pio had no sooner entered, than he saw him.

'Genoese,' he cried above everyone's head, 'Genoese, you have a dirty face! You live so near the sea, how come you don't know how to wash yourself?'

We can imagine the poor fellow's consternation. Everyone stared at him, naturally, and Padre Pio did not desist: 'Your boat is solid, but no one is at the helm The incident, of course, ended in the confessional, to Padre Pio's great joy.

In speaking of Alberto Del Fante, Maria Winowska says that anyone who has written about Padre Pio has raided his book, *The Story of Padre Pio of Pietrelcina*, and that many books which are bought abroad are nothing more than simple paragraphs from this precious document. Well, Alberto Del Fante, himself, was one of Padre Pio's great trophies. Like so many others, he had started out by fighting him in a series of vehement articles which appeared in his *Secular Italy*, and in which he accused the Capuchin stigmatist of being 'a fraud, a charlatan, and a rogue who took advantage of the ignorance of a credulous and ingenuous people'.

Heaven sent him an answer, soon enough, in the form of the remarkably indisputable curing of one of his nephews, who had been gravely ill. Unbeknownst to him, a friend had simply asked the 'impostor' of San Giovanni Rotondo to cure him, and within twenty-four hours, to the amazement of the doctors, the young man was cured.

Alberto Del Fante, who was much disturbed, decided to go and see this strange miracle worker himself. To be clear and precise, each day he wrote down his impressions. 'Fraud or saint?' he wondered from the moment he arrived in San Giovanni Rotondo. Padre Pio looked like 'an ordinary friar', and he felt a vehement desire to doubt him.

'I went to confession, told everything, but without

enthusiasm, without faith; I thought that I was dealing with a very ordinary priest. He differed from the others in only one respect: he knew everything. He knew my sins; he told me that I had belonged to a society that recognises God, but dislikes his ministers.

'He probably guessed that I was a Mason, perhaps from the entire conversation since we discussed at length a little philosophy and men who although lacking faith, are guided by their conscience. We spoke of St Augustine, of Spinoza, of Descartes, of Stuart Mill, of Spencer, of Darwin and of modern philosophers.

'"Padre," I said "my actions have always been honest, and if sometimes the beast triumphed over the man, my conscience would say, 'Do this; don't do that ... do that ... I have never had faith, yet I have always been honest.'"

'"Honest? Even when ...?" He told me things that he had no way of knowing.'

Alberto Del Fante finally surrendered, and being a righteous person, he did so seriously, and forever. This was one of Padre Pio's greatest joys.

Once, in a group of women who were waiting for Padre Pio to pass, there happened to be one of loose morals. Padre Pio, with his supernatural intuition, spoke gently: 'Will the one among you who has had the courage to follow Mary Magdalene in sin, please have the strength to follow her in penance. Anyone who has fallen in mud can still be saved if she has the will.'

Upon hearing these words, one of the group fell to her knees, asking forgiveness, and promised to start a new life.

Another testimony of faith was that of Luisa Vairo, a very wealthy and beautiful young lady. She had come to San Giovanni Rotondo (wrote Winowska) purely out of curiosity, and also to defy public opinion.

No sooner had she arrived than she felt invaded by a sharp pain; her sins seemed so monstrous, so hideous, that she unashamedly burst into tears right in the church.

Her heart-rending sobs attracted the attention of some spiritual daughter of the Padre. Padre Pio was hearing confessions, but as soon as he was informed, he approached Miss Vairo and said: 'Be calm, my dear. God's compassion is unlimited, and the blood of Jesus Christ washes away all the sins of the world.'

'I want to confess my sins,' said the unknown lady, who would have laughed at such a proposition an hour ago.

'First calm yourself,' said the Padre gently; 'You can return tomorrow.'

Miss Vairo spent the entire night reviewing her sins. She hadn't been to confession since childhood!

Like so many others, she felt completely dismayed in Padre Pio's presence. There was no way of getting out of it; she felt as if a rope were tightening around her neck.

Seeing her in such a pitiful state, Padre Pio gently began to make an inventory of her sad life. Finally, he said to her, 'Don't you remember anything else?'

A vehement temptation caused her to tremble. Was it really necessary to confess that remaining big sin? Wasn't this exposition of shame and mud sufficient? Padre Pio was waiting, gently moving his lips. Finally, she recovered. 'There is still one more, dear Father.'

'God be praised!' he happily exclaimed. 'That's what I was waiting for. I will give you absolution, my dear.'

That day when Padre Pio left the confessional, his face was radiant with joy. He had conquered another soul for Jesus.

When Miss Vairo was converted, she followed the example of the great penitents with the ardour of all neophytes. One winter morning, she decided to walk to church in her bare feet. It was a cold, windy, rainy day, typical of the Gargano. Soaked to the skin, her feet bleeding from the sharp stones that in those days lay on the road, she fainted in the doorway of the church, no longer able to tolerate the pain and the cold.

When she revived, Padre Pio was bending over her. 'My dear, we shouldn't go beyond our limits, not even in holy penance,' he said. Then gently touching her shoulder he added, 'Fortunately this water does not wet.' Imagine the amazement of all those who were present when they realised that in the blink of an eye, Miss Vairo's clothes became completely dry!

Two more conversions that resounded through Emilia-Romagna and all of Italy were the conversions of Carlo Lusardi of Modena, and of Italia Betti of Bologna. Both of them were determined, practising Marxists, and later two pearls of joy for Padre Pio.

On 7 September 1933, according to Fr Fernando of Riese, Carlo Lusardi was leaving Pescara, heading for San Giovanni Rotondo. His turbid past and 'a mysterious voice' urged him on.

He was born in Bologna in 1900, to non-practising parents. He spent his childhood in Nice, and then returned to Bologna at the age of fifteen, a non-believer. In 1923 he enrolled in the Communist Party, which at that time was illegal. In 1925, he married, but had only a civil ceremony. He was employed by a publishing firm, met with instant success, and bought two companies – one in Modena, the other in Pescara. He left his wife, and was living with another woman.

In 1933, financial reverses cast him into the gutter. Psychologically destroyed, he decided to commit suicide. While he was walking towards the railroad where he intended to put this drastic plan into effect, he met Prof. Manelli, who was returning from San Giovanni Rotondo. When the professor spoke to him about Padre Pio, Lusardi felt a strong desire to see him. He left immediately. On the train, he made a general confession in writing.

The next morning he met Padre Pio in the sacristy after Mass. He tried to kiss the Padre's hand, but the Padre pulled it back, and looked at him severely. Lusardi had the feeling that the Padre already knew all about him. That night, wanting to see the Padre, he waited for him to finish his prayers in the choir loft. It was then that a tremendous crisis caused him to sob desperately. Upon presenting himself to Padre Pio, he managed to say, 'Father, I'm a poor wretch. Have pity on me!'

The Padre simply replied, 'Tell me all about it, my son.'

On his knees, Lusardi bared his soul. Then he heard the Padre say, 'Validate your marriage with a religious ceremony; straighten out your life, and come back soon. Go … God bless you.'

Lusardi succinctly concludes, 'This is the story of my conversion from Marxism to Catholicism.'

On 14 December 1949, Italia Betti, a mathematics teacher at Galvani High School in Bologna, was on her way to Padre Pio's friary. Anyone who knew her would know that this was a very strange, inexplicable decision for her to make. In the political milieu of Bologna, she was known as a first rate Communist: provincial secretary of the Italian Women's Union; political agitator; determined and indefatigable propagandist for Marxism–Leninism in the cities and outskirts of Emilia; a most active director of the Communist faction. She had been urged by Padre Pio himself, whom she had seen in a dream, to take this trip. In the little Church of Santa Maria delle Grazie, Miss Betti, who was quite ill, felt strangely mystified when she saw Padre Pio at the altar celebrating Mass.

The next morning, after a sleepless night, the teacher jumped in front of Padre Pio's confessional, and in public, before everyone, loudly denounced the ideology of Communism; she added that she wished to return to God. To the principal of Galvani High School in Bologna, to her fellow teachers, and to some of her students, she wrote: 'I have found peace. Pray for me.'

By no means could anyone make her change her mind. A few of her companions tried everything possible, but failed. Miss Betti flatly refused to leave San Giovanni Rotondo. She wanted to remain there, close to the priest who had brought her back to God, who showed her the road to peace after twenty years of floundering. There she died, a victim of cancer, on 26 October 1950. She is buried in the little cemetery, in accordance with her wishes, wearing the cord of a Franciscan Tertiary.

Fr Fernando Neopolitano wonders how many times Padre Pio had the secret joy of bringing back a prodigal son or daughter. No one will ever know their number or their story. The secrets of their souls will never be revealed, particularly because their confessor never divulged anything about those who returned to God. In humility and in solitude, he thanked the Lord for this joy.

Hidden on the lower part of the Gargano, near the plateau, the little church of his friary seemed like a miniature seaport where many souls arrived, exhausted from their stormy crossing. They conquered, often with fear in their hearts, the rough sea.

Prodigious Cures

Several hundred thousand people have passed through the city of Foggia and through San Severo, asking for directions to San Giovanni Rotondo.

Millions of eyes have fastened, and are still fastened, on the spur of Italy, on that promontory called the Gargano. Its natural, untamed beauty, almost unaltered through the ages, is saturated with provocative poetry which stirs the senses in a startling, seductive, and bewitching manner.

In this small area, one can admire panoramic landscapes which are an amalgamation of the various characteristics of the most beautiful localities of Italy: the forests of Aosta Valley, the orange groves of Sicily, the vineyards of the environs of Rome, the Carnic crags, the olive groves of Tuscany, the valleys of Umbria, the sea coast of Liguria, the coastal cliffs of Sorrento, the melancholy beauty of Maremma, the white rock of the Carnic mountains, the ravines of the Dolomites, the lakes of Trentino, and the woodlands of Sardinia.

San Giovanni Rotondo is located in the middle of the Gargano, on a lovely plateau at the foot of the highest hill of the Garganic range, Mount Calvo (1,056 metres). It is surrounded by fertile land (much of which is abandoned today) where cereals, vegetables, almonds, and olives are cultivated. It was once noted for its pastures; the shepherds of the time were all intimate friends of Padre Pio. Since 1918, this little village has had the world in an uproar; it was privileged to become the adopted village of the stigmatist, Padre Pio of Pietrelcina, and in a few short years, its fame had spread to all five continents.

Today, speaking of San Giovanni Rotondo means speaking of Padre Pio, of that friar who lived his true life only when he was in solitude, away from the world, and in perpetual prayer; the friar who bore the symbols of Christ crucified.

This little village which was once unknown and abandoned, is now recognised as a place which gives peace and serenity to tormented souls, and health to weakened bodies; it becomes a fatherland to anyone who feels lost.

Before setting out on the road to hope, everyone wonders: 'What is happening on the Gargano; why is everyone talking about San Giovanni Rotondo? Could it be fanaticism?' But how can it be fanaticism when, along with the populace, one finds kings, princes, heads of state, generals, cardinals, bishops, actors, sportsmen, industrialists, and the most famous and renowned scientists. They have all come here to the Gargano mountain to lay their spiritual burden at the wounded feet of a Franciscan friar. They have come here to confess their sins, to cry, to implore him to raise his wounded hand, and like Jesus, bring health back to so many suffering minds, bodies and souls. This is certainly not fanaticism. As a matter of fact, one might say that if Padre Pio had done nothing else, by this means alone he would have accomplished the most important and valid obligation of his mission, because, according to the chronicles, men truly come, cry, and return home happy and renewed.

The Gargano is a living chronicle: 'As long as Padre Pio leads souls to God,' declared Pope Benedict XV, 'it is my duty to stay close to him.'

Padre Pio had the gift of consoling with a mere glance; his supernatural energy sparkled in his mobile, penetrating eyes. He would hardly reach the doorway, than his eyes would begin searching for anguished, unhappy, pre-occupied souls; and in a silent exchange of glances, troubles disappeared. So very often, he merely held out his hand to be kissed, and every affliction vanished. What was his secret? He knew how to renounce the world in order to live a life of prayer and suffering. And it was precisely his life of prayer and suffering that made him worthy of conquering the people of the world. It was for their benefit that he prayed and suffered, for their benefit that he obtained cures from God.

Often the press spoke of the cures obtained by people who went to the Stigmatist of the Gargano; newspapers and magazines were full of these stories. It is true that some of them were exaggerated and glorified for economic reasons; however, if all the real and documented cures were included in this little book there would not be enough space.

The following example is especially noteworthy because it deals with surgery; it cannot be attributed to auto-suggestion.

Miss Giuseppina Marchetti of Bologna, aged twenty-four, had fractured her right arm. That same arm had been injured in a serious accident three years previous, and she had had to undergo surgery. After a second operation, which was followed by long, painful therapy, the surgeon told the young lady's father that she would never regain the use of her arm. It was completely ankylosed after the removal of a part of her shoulder blade, and unfortunately, there was no articulation of the bone structure.

Devastated, both father and daughter left for San Giovanni Rotondo. Padre Pio received them, blessed them, and declared: 'Above all, no despondency! Have faith in the Lord! The arm will heal.' It was the end of July 1930. The sick girl returned to Bologna without even the slightest sign of improvement. No doubt, Padre Pio was mistaken! She put it out of her mind – and the months passed.

On 17 September, the day of the stigmata of St Francis, suddenly the Marchetti's apartment was permeated with the delightful scent of jonquils and roses. The phenomenon lasted about a quarter of an hour, while the surprised tenants searched in vain for its origin. Although she did not know it at the time, the cures obtained through the intercession of Padre Pio are often preceded by his characteristic waves of perfume.

On that day, the girl regained the use of her arm. An x-ray, which she treasured, shows the restoration of the bone and cartilage.

The next incident is taken from Alberto Del Fante's book. 'At the beginning of the year 1921, Mother Teresa Salvadores,

In the Friary Garden
Padre Pio takes a brief pause from his intense apostolic ministry to stroll in
the friary's garden, under cypresses and in the shade of pines.

Superior of the Miraculous Medal Atelier School of Montevideo, Uruguay, developed a critical cardiac condition with cardio-aortic lesions. Serious gastric disturbances resulting from cancer of the stomach (according to one of the doctors in attendance) made her condition so grave that she became bedridden. For even the slightest action, she had to be helped by one of the sisters. She could no longer tolerate any nourishment, and was kept alive by means of injections and morphine.

'Having heard of Padre Pio, the sisters, who loved their Mother Superior very dearly, wrote to him in November 1921, imploring his intercession for the sick woman.

'By this time her strength was completely depleted, and her life was ending; she had even rejected the morphine injections and was waiting for death to end her torment.

'In the meantime, the sisters were visited by a lady, a relative of Mgr Damiani, Vicar of the Diocese of Saito, Uruguay. Mgr Damiani had just returned from Italy and had brought back from San Giovanni Rotondo, a glove that Padre Pio had worn.

'"The glove was applied to me," says Mother Teresa, herself, "first to my side where I had a swelling the size of a fist; then to my throat where I felt suffocated. Then I fell asleep. In my dream I saw Padre Pio; he touched my side where the pain was, breathed into my mouth, and told me so many things that are not of this world. The fact is, that after three hours, I woke up, asked for my habit so that I could get out of the bed in which I had been lying for three months ... I got up without anyone's help, and went down to the chapel … At noon I went to the refectory, and I, who hadn't eaten for so long, ate more than my sisters … From that day, I have had no further illness."'

The doctor who attended the sister, Prof. Giambattista Morelli of the University of Montevideo, wrote a scholarly report on the case. Later, he went to Italy to visit Padre Pio, and returned to South America full of faith.

In the early part of 1925, Mrs Paolina Preziosi, a mother of five children, a Franciscan tertiary, became so gravely ill with pneumonia that the attending doctor could do nothing for her. Friends and relatives of the sick woman ran to Padre Pio asking his intercession for her. To the crying women, Padre Pio replied, 'Tell her to have no fear since she will be resurrected with our Lord.'

It was Friday night of Holy Week. The poor woman was praying to God that her life be spared for the sake of her five children, when suddenly Padre Pio appeared to her. 'Have no fear,' he said, 'Creature of God, have no fear. Have faith and hope; tomorrow, when the bells ring, you will be cured.'

During the night, however, the poor woman was in a coma, so her relatives prepared the habit in order to dress her as soon as she died.

On Sunday morning, at the sound of the bells announcing the Risen Christ, Mrs. Preziosi jumped out of bed as if she had been pushed by a superhuman force; she made her thanksgiving to God and to the Padre, praising and thanking them with a heart full of gratitude.

There is hardly a soul in San Giovanni Rotondo who doesn't know the tale of Dr Francesco Ricciardi. He was a militant atheist, who for many years had conducted a campaign of defamation against religion, and against the Capuchin stigmatist. Padre Pio, who was aware of it, suffered in silence. But finally the hour of reprisal arrived. 'God's friends,' says Winowska, 'have a way with vengeance.'

Dr Ricciardi became ill. His colleagues, Dr Giuva, Dr Morcaldi, Dr Mauricelli, Dr Merla, and Dr Capuano made the following diagnosis: cancer of the stomach, too late for an operation. Soon the news spread that Dr Ricciardi was dying.

He was well-liked in the town even though he was an atheist, because he had a generous heart and treated the poor free of charge.

The Archpriest, Don Giuseppe Prencipe, took his courage in hand, and went to see Dr Ricciardi. 'I don't want any priests,' shouted the sick man angrily, and to prove his point, he threw his slipper right in Fr Prencipe's face. Not at all discouraged, Don Giuseppe insisted. 'Leave me in peace!' shouted the doctor. 'Only to Padre Pio would I make my confession. But I have offended him too much for him to come. Besides, he is unable to leave the friary. Therefore, I shall die as I have lived. Enough!'

Dr Angelo Maria Merla, who had once been an atheist himself, ran to inform Padre Pio. The Padre quickly entered the church, took the Holy Oils and the Viaticum, and, limping on his wounded feet, hurried to the doctor. Outside, the wind was howling furiously; heavy sleet was falling on Padre Pio, who was meditating on his God all the while, holding Him close to his heart.

As soon as he arrived, the Padre opened his arms in an affectionate gesture, and smiled that boyish smile which was so characteristic of him.

The old non-believer stared at him, stupefied. His face brightened as he said, 'Forgive me, Padre Pio!' The atheist was conquered; the atheist bowed his head as he had never wanted to bow it; the atheist made the sign of the cross and joined his hands in prayer.

He made his confession, was forgiven, received the Sacrament of the Anointing of the Sick, then received Holy Communion. He should have died peacefully, but then the 'vengeance of the saints' would not have been complete; at Padre Pio's request, God decided differently.

After three days, the doctor was cured. The cancer disappeared without leaving a single trace. Completely restored, the old opponent did a complete turnabout, and fought Padre Pio's adversaries.

The documentation of cures obtained through Padre Pio's prayers is extremely long, but we will briefly mention just a few more.

Pasquale Di Chiara, Chancellor of the district court of San Giovanni Rotondo, was barely able to drag his left leg after a fall. One day, he heard Padre Pio say, 'Throw away the cane and walk.' Miraculously, he was then able to walk without help. One of his children, aged three, had infantile paralysis, and at Padre Pio's command disposed of his orthopaedic apparatus as well – he too was able to walk!

Similarly, Pasquale Urbano of Foggia, was also hardly able to walk after a fall from a carriage. Medical treatment was worthless. One day, after hearing his confession, Padre

Pio said to him, 'Get up and go! Throw away that cane.' And so he did!

Antonio D'Onofrio of Foggia, a victim of typhus at the age of four, became a hunchback. One day, after hearing his confession, Padre Pio patted his distorted back, and the boy straightened up, his hunch gone.

Grazia Siena, who was born blind, was able to see after twenty-nine years of blindness, thanks to Padre Pio's prayers.

Countess Oliva Baiocchi was cured of a tumour on the left side of her abdomen; Maria Gozzi, of Ghizzano, Pisa, was cured of epithelioma of the tongue in 1919.

Giuseppe Canaponi of Sarteano was hit by a car while driving a motorcycle. He was taken to the Rizzoli Ortho-paedic Institute of Bologna with a broken thigh bone, and for three years his leg remained rigid. His wife and son accompanied him to San Giovanni Rotondo. When he came before Padre Pio for confession, unaware of what he was doing, he knelt down, bending the knee that had been rigid and ankylosed for three years. He got up without the help of his cane and walked quickly, to the amazement of his wife and son and acquaintances. The director of the Orthopaedic Hospital of the University of Siena, Leopoldo Giuntini, made the following declaration: 'The instant recovery of articular movement in the case of Canaponi cannot be explained within the limits of our present knowledge.'

Those are just some of the prodigious cures, and there are hundreds more, especially those that have taken place after the Padre's death.

It couldn't be more clear that Padre Pio felt a tremendous responsibility for all those who had come before him for help. He always said, 'I shall never forget anyone who comes to me.' To one of his spiritual sons he said, 'My son, you think you know how much I care for you, but my affection for you is greater than you can imagine. I follow you with my prayers, with my suffering, and with my tears. I want you to know that my heart is always with you, that I will never abandon you for any reason.'

The Padre gave every spiritual son or daughter a measure of caresses, smiles, advice, prayers, sacrifices, and even reprimands. No one was ever denied what was necessary for their spiritual or physical existence.

The Prayer Groups

In addition to the Home for the Relief of Suffering, Padre Pio's heart and mind conceived another gem which he gave to the Church and to all humanity: the Prayer Groups.

During World War II, Pope Pius XII's numerous appeals to prayer effectively found a prompt reply in Padre Pio's heart. 'Let's do something about it,' he said to a small group of spiritual children who were with him at that moment. 'Let's roll up our sleeves and be the first to respond to the appeal of our Roman Pontiff.'

This is how the Prayer Groups were born.

The nature of the Community Prayer Group movement was defined by Padre Pio, himself, in an oration delivered on 5 May 1966: 'The cultivation of faith; the germination of love, where Christ, Himself, will be present at every prayer meeting; the fraternal agape under the guidance of a pastor or spiritual director.'

The Padre's children quickly responded to the call, so that here and there across the country, they gathered together in churches to pray. The prayer groups so desired by the Pope were now established. Prayer in solitude changed to community prayer. It was a spontaneous act, a natural, fraternal desire to occasionally meet under one roof in the Lord's House.

It was nothing exceptional. Nothing different from what other Christians were doing. It was only that they felt more united. They attended Mass, and prayed aloud for the individual or general intentions of the group. Their intentions were united to those of the Holy Pontiff and of Padre Pio.

The official appeal for the formation of Prayer Groups was made in every city, in every town, during the month of August 1950.

'It is time to unite! It is time to unite both intentions and actions: *To offer* our Lord collective prayers imploring His mercy for a humanity that appears to have forgotten Him; *to feel* in the collective participation of the Divine Sacrifice of the Mass the wonderful mystery of love that Jesus bestows on humanity for their redemption; *to adore* God in the most Holy Sacrament – the greatest mystery of our faith, the marvellous gift which God has given humanity for their salvation, for their elevation towards Him who is their Father; to live in a state of Grace so as to feel like God's own children.'

During Padre Pio's lifetime, the movement had extended so far that they were already holding regional, national, and international conventions.

In Italy, the first regional convention was held in Venice on 6 May 1956; the first national convention was held in Catania on 12 September 1959, under the chairmanship of Cardinal Giacomo Lercaro. The international convention was held in San Giovanni Rotondo on 20 September 1968, under the watchful eye of our beloved Padre.

In July 1968, several months before Padre Pio's death, there arrived a notice which was the equivalent of an official recognition and approval of the Prayer Groups on the part of the Church.

As a matter of fact, in a document dated 31 July 1968, signed by the Most Eminent Prefect Cardinal Ildebrando Antoniutti, the Sacred Congregation for Religious and Secular Institutions entrusted the establishment and coordination of Prayer Groups to the Guardian of the Friary of San Giovanni Rotondo.

This formal recognition comforted Padre Pio during his last days, and Cardinal Giacomo Lercaro remarked: 'On the vigil of his death, Padre Pio, who had quietly nourished the Prayer Groups, finally saw the supreme approval of them. In a chorus of prayers, his earthly mission ended. In reality, his mission had been a continuous prayer, a persistent supplication to our Heavenly Father to give him, with Christ, in Christ, for Christ, the needs, the pains, the hopes, the anxieties of the Church and of the entire world.'

On 20 September 1968, the anniversary of Padre Pio's stigmata, the Vatican newspaper, *L'Osservatore Romano*, published a brief account of the Prayer Groups: 'At present, there are 726 Groups, 668 of which are in Italy, 21 in France, 8 in Australia, 6 in Switzerland, 5 in Belgium, 5 in the United States, 3 in Germany, 2 in Luxembourg, 1 in the Principality of Monaco, 1 in Morocco, 1 in South Africa, 1 in Tunisia, 1 in Turkey, 1 in El Salvador and 1 in Chile ...

'The movement, initiated by Padre Pio of Pietrelcina, now has about 68,000 members who meet at least once a month to offer their community prayers for the intentions of Padre Pio.

'Every group has as a spiritual director, a priest approved by the Bishop of the diocese. Of the 276 present spiritual directors, 544 are diocesan priests, 124 belong to various religious orders and congregations, 58 belong to the Capuchin Order.'

By 1 March 1976, there were more than 1,400 groups with more than 150,000 members and sympathisers.

This great movement which was born in Padre Pio's heart, has grown to be a tremendous chorus which links Heaven to earth, and men to God; it harmonises angel voices with human voices, Heavenly music with earthly music; it brings peace to man's heart in the love of God, and God's loving hand to the hearts of men.

The Crucible of Tribulation

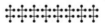

After the dazzling sunshine, after the marvellous construction of the Home for the Relief of Suffering, after the establishment of Prayer Groups, gloom appeared on the horizon in the form of intensely unpleasant surprises which caused poor Padre Pio to exclaim: 'We are at the last station, the longest and the most painful.'

After World War II, the influx of the faithful continued to increase, giving Padre Pio's good works a chance to shine even brighter. However, the crowds that gathered in the square and in the church were sometimes disorderly and noisy. News was often divulged without the permission of responsible authority, causing misunderstandings, equivocations, and misconceptions in regard to Padre Pio and his work. It resulted in disagreeable repercussions, and caused a good deal of suffering and bitterness.

It might be said that the years between 1952 and 1962 were a period of conflict and upheaval which visibly influenced the life of Padre Pio. Afflictions that would have shattered even cast iron, fell upon him in rapid succession, keeping him in a state of perpetual anxiety, pushing him to the limits of human endurance. But the Padre was not resentful. He accepted every restriction with tremendous patience, humility, and confidence. He never uttered an angry word, not even in private. In addition, he happily took other people's troubles and made them his own.

According to Luigi Tucci, he lived this way for a long time; alone, but in harmony with nature. At noon, from his little open window he would listen to the profound silence, broken only by a gust of wind, or the flutter of a wing. And though he could not banish the inertia which plagued him, even on the most dismal of days, he would continue to pray, burning that extraneous feeling in the flame of his faith.

As was to be expected, the clamour of the press resulted in the intervention of the ecclesiastic authorities, and of the Capuchin Order. The Church did not delay in breaking its silence. It had the right, and availed itself of that right with its customary sagacity.

On 31 December 1951, Mgrs Giovanni Pepe and Emanuele Caronti, prelates of the Holy Office, arrived in San Giovanni Rotondo and quickly set to work. Experienced and wise, both men asked questions, investigated, evaluated, verified, and took everything into account. However, they made no decisions.

On 16 January 1952, Fr Angelo of Genoa arrived in the capacity of inspector, having been sent by the Minister General of the Capuchin Order.

On 11 March and 8 April 1952, the Holy Office subjected the Minister General of the Capuchins to 'a few inconveniences' encountered at San Giovanni Rotondo.

On 6 July 1952, quite unexpectedly, Fr Benigo of Sant'Ilario Milan, General of the Order, arrived. He had previously, on 3 May 1952, dissuaded priests from planning pilgrimages to San Giovanni Rotondo, and from distributing publications and pictures about Padre Pio.

On 3 August 1952, the Vatican newspaper, *L'Osservatore Romano*, published a decree of the Holy Office, proscribing eight publications about Padre Pio which lacked the necessary ecclesiastic revision and approval. Although it was expressly said that the declaration did not imply 'a condemnation of Padre Pio, nor of the authors of the books', this act embittered people, and created an atmosphere of diffidence.

On 15 December 1954, the Minister General of the Order imposed this restriction on Padre Pio: 'Do not concern yourself with controversies that arise among the members of the Home for the Relief of Suffering.'

On 21 December 1954, it was rumoured that the Superiors wanted to transfer Padre Pio from San Giovanni Rotondo; this rumour irritated the hearts of the citizens.

The gloom worsened. In the angry minds of certain people, even the most absurd things seemed true. Fortunately, Padre Pio's outward calm succeeded in assuaging most fears.

Many things were said, often controversial. Many people participated, including those with vivid imaginations, and those who cannot help but spread discord. It was said, for instance, that several friars of the friary were to be transferred, that the Capuchins had impelled the Vatican to appoint a new 'apostolic inspector' who would remain outside the jurisdiction of the Holy Office, etc.

The truth is that on 30 July 1960, Mgr Carlo Maccari of the Congregational Assembly arrived in San Giovanni Rotondo as the apostolic inspector of the friary, and the Home for the Relief of Suffering. The visit, which was to go on until 17 September of that same year, was highly publicised by the press whose judgement was imprudent and indiscreet.

It was almost the eve of Padre Pio's sacerdotal golden anniversary, so Mgr Maccari began his work by holding a press conference in one of the rooms of the Home for the Relief of Suffering, to disclose the essential reason for his visit. He revised and simplified the programme of festivities in honour of the Padre, and made some notations for the Mayor in regard to what was written on the placards, among other things.

This first attempt did not succeed in pleasing a good number of 'devotees', especially because the Padre's spiritual dignity was always outstanding in every respect; he never fell apart, never faltered for a moment in the face of adversity. He always remained calm, resigned and fully submissive to the plans of Rome, which for him were also God's plans. Without losing his composure, he continued to wholeheartedly give hope to the souls who were in need of it.

One of the first provisions of Mgr Maccari was to change the Guardian of the Friary; thus Fr Rosario of Aliminusa, a good friar, but also competent and decisive, quickly left Sicily to take the place of Fr Emilio of Matrice.

Other provisions followed, but the memory of them has been eradicated by time. However, in the midst of so much pain and suffering, there came a messenger from Providence. On 20 June 1960, on the eve of his sacerdotal golden anniversary, he received a very warm letter from a first rate Cardinal, the one who was to occupy Peter's Chair, and bear the name of Paul VI. It read:

> Most Venerable Father, I hear that you will soon celebrate the fiftieth anniversary of your ordination to the priesthood; I shall try, therefore, to express in the Lord, my congratulations for the immense graces that have been bestowed upon you, and which have been dispensed by you. Happy and grateful for the Lord's goodness, I repeat this appropriate quotation: *Venite, audite et narrabo, omnes qui timetis Deum, quanta fecit animae meae!* (Come, listen and I will tell you, all you who love the Lord, what wonders He has worked in my soul.) That is how the Priesthood should be celebrated. What can we say about yours, which was favoured by so many gifts and so much fecundity!
>
> I also express the hope that our Lord Jesus will continue to live and to manifest Himself in you, and in your ministry. As St Paul says: 'The life of Christ is manifested in our mortal flesh.'
>
> I know that you pray for me. I need your prayers very much; please recommend to the Lord this diocese, and your most devoted,
>
> Cardinal Montini, Archbishop of Milan.

In regard to the influx of the faithful, and to the progress of affairs, Fr Rosario declared: 'Everyday we have to deal with throngs of diversified people, so that in spite of our vigilance and precautions, we sometimes cannot prevent some small inconvenience … In every crowd we can expect to find those who are truly pious and those who come solely out of curiosity. Anyone familiar with our assignment will easily realise how much patience is required of us at every moment, and how much we are exposed to recrimination.

'It is physically impossible to please everyone when everyone is asking for the same thing – to confer with Padre Pio for various reasons, and at all hours of the day. Frankly, it is a task which tires us, and makes us weary … Even I, after three years, feel tired … My fatigue truly increases when I have to sustain that of my fellow priests!'

After these turbulent years, a serious loss caused Padre Pio considerable pain: the death of Fr Agostino of San Marco in Lamis, his spiritual director. He died on 14 May 1963.

Padre Pio's Aroma

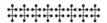

During his lifetime, St Joseph of Cupertino, a spiritual son of St Francis of Assisi, had many attributes and experiences that paralleled those of our Padre Pio of Pietrelcina. Among them were his great love for God and for souls; his apostolate for the confessional; the ecstasies; the scrutinising of consciences; bilocation; misunderstandings and persecutions on the part of higher authority; and even that special mystical phenomenon which made his clothes, the objects he used, and his cell, diffuse an incomparable perfume that was sweet and fragrant.

In this chapter, we will speak of the odour of sanctity that emanated from Padre Pio.

Our most reliable and authentic sources include Dr Giorgio Festa and Dr Luigi Romanelli who were trustworthy persons charged by the ecclesiastical authorities to examine Padre Pio's wounds.

In his book, *Mystery of Science and Light of Faith*, Dr Festa declared: 'The drops of blood issuing from the wounds of Padre Pio's body have a fine, delicate aroma; many people who approach him are distinctly aware of it ... Padre Pio does not use, and has never used, any kind of perfume, yet many who get close to him ascertain that a pleasant scent emanates from his body. It seems to be a mixture of violets and roses.

'What is the source of that scent?

'In matters that concern me, I can only affirm that on my first visit, I removed a blood-soaked cloth from his side. I brought it back with me to examine under the microscope. I, personally, for reasons already stated [Dr Festa didn't have a sense of smell], did not perceive any special scent; however, a distinguished officer, and other persons who were riding in my car on the return trip from San Giovanni Rotondo, smelled the fragrance and assured me that it was precisely the scent that emanated from Padre Pio's body. These people were unaware of the fact that I had the cloth with me, enclosed in a case. They were able to perceive the fragrance in spite of the fact that the fast moving car was well ventilated.

'In Rome, I placed the cloth in a cabinet. For a long period of time its fragrance permeated my office so thoroughly, that many people who came to consult me spontaneously asked about the origin of the fragrance.

'Many people who have recently been to San Giovanni Rotondo have had the same experience. So did my colleague Dr Romanelli who accompanied me on my second visit to Padre Pio, and whose sense of smell is normal.'

Here is the express opinion of Dr Luigi Romanelli, head doctor of the Civil Hospital of Barletta. In a letter to the Minister Provincial of that time, Fr Pietro of Ischitella, he wrote: 'I have read the report written by Dr Festa. It clearly indicates that he is a scrupulous observer, a noteworthy scientist and a just critic.

'Every now and then I hear about the fragrance. I recall that even I noticed that scent, and if you will permit me to say so, I enjoyed it. On my first trip to San Giovanni Rotondo in June 1919, I was no sooner presented to Padre Pio than I noticed a certain fragrance that emanated from his body. I told the Most Reverend E. E. of Valenzano, who was with me, that I didn't think it suitable for a friar to use perfume, especially a friar who was so well esteemed.

'During the remaining two days in San Giovanni Rotondo, I did not notice any aroma, even though I had visited Padre Pio in his cell. In the afternoon, just before my departure, while I was going down the stairs, all of a sudden I noticed the same scent that I had perceived on the first day; it lasted but a few moments.

'Most Reverend Father, please note that it was not my imagination. First of all, no one had ever told me about this phenomenon; secondly, if it had been my imagination, I would have noticed that scent frequently, rather than occasionally. I wanted to make this declaration because, too often, we tend to attribute to the imagination, phenomena that are difficult to explain, or that cannot be explained.'

The phenomenon of the aroma has made many a non-believer laugh, and has been the cause of many discussions, as were the stigmata. During the years, the number of witnesses of this scent has grown, and this strange phenomenon can no longer be doubted. Its significance, however, is still being debated.

This phenomenon of the aroma, which is manifested even now after Padre Pio's death, usually comes in waves, and is perceived by everyone who is present. Sometimes it vanishes gradually; at other times it lingers persistently. Sometimes some people perceive it while others do not, even though they may be together in the same location.

From experience, we know that the scent is proof of Padre Pio's spiritual presence when he wishes to help, guide, or warn someone. It is especially present in the case of a cure, a conversion, or when a grave decision has to be made. It is quite often a deciding factor in the lives of certain individuals. At other times, it is simply a warning, as it was in the case of a poor woman in San Giovanni Rotondo. She was walking backwards while picking chestnuts at the top of a mountain, when suddenly she became aware of the significant smell of violets; turning around, she discovered a precipice behind her.

Often the phenomenon was manifested to groups of friends, or spiritual children of Padre Pio who were discussing him. It was as if, like Jesus, he wanted to fulfil the promise to be present when at least three devotees are united in prayer.

More often, Padre Pio's aroma was the affirmative reply to a requested grace, as in the case of the accountant Laderachi of Cosenza. The latter had seriously injured his head in a fall from a truck, and lay agonising in a hospital. In the chapel of the hospital, his wife and friends were fervently praying, imploring Padre Pio's aid. Suddenly a wave of strong perfume, 'like a blooming shrub', permeated the chapel. Padre Pio was answering them! Their hope was renewed, and their hearts filled with gratitude.

'How can it be an illusion', wrote Piera Delfino Sessa, 'when it happens unexpectedly and in distant places? It is most amazing how it is perceived in cities that are far from San Giovanni Rotondo, like Genoa, Milan, Venice – and even abroad. It happens when it is least expected, when there is no apparent means of producing it. How much easier it is to understand that the Padre's clothes or sacred vestments may emit a fragrance, than his perfume should reach a person who is travelling, or a person whom he doesn't even know, or reach a non-believer, which sometimes happens. This is what amazes and perplexes everyone. But why should we be amazed if God wants to manifest Himself to us through a simple mortal, particularly if that mortal is very dear to Him?'

In regard to this, we will mention an episode whose validity of proof, according to Maria Winowska, stems from the fact that the witnesses knew nothing about Padre Pio's scent.

A young Polish couple residing in England had to make a serious decision. After reflecting at length on the 'pros and cons', they found themselves in a terrible dilemma.

Their situation appeared to be desperate. What could they do? Someone spoke to them about Padre Pio. They wrote to him. No answer! So they decided to go to San Giovanni Rotondo to ask his advice in person.

It was a long distance from England to San Giovanni Rotondo. Our travellers first stopped in Berne, Switzerland,

and anxiously asked each other whether it was worth the bother to continue. There was always the possibility that the Padre would not receive them – before they left, someone had told them that he was 'sequestered'. All the travelling, all the expense, would be useless.

It was evening. They were having a discussion in the attic room of a cheap hotel, which they had rented in order to economise. It was winter; it was snowing, and they were cold and discouraged. They were on the verge of turning back, when all of a sudden they became enveloped in a strong, exquisite perfume. It was so pleasant that they felt compensated for their efforts.

The young woman began to inspect the bureau and the closet to find some bottle of perfume that had been left behind by a forgetful traveller, but the search was in vain. After a while the perfume vanished, and the room smelled damp and dank once more.

Confused, our travellers questioned the owner of the hotel, who was amazed by this story! It was the first time that the guests of his hotel (which had hardly been sprinkled with rose water) believed to have smelled perfume. Nevertheless, the experience animated them, so they decided to continue the trip – come what may.

When they arrived in San Giovanni Rotondo, they went quickly to Padre Pio. He received them with open arms. The young man, who could speak Italian, stammered: 'We wrote to you, Father; why didn't you answer us?'

'What do you mean, I didn't answer you? That night at the Swiss hotel, didn't you smell anything?' With a few words, he solved their problem and took leave of them.

They were brimming with joy and gratitude. They were also delighted to learn about Padre Pio's 'method of correspondence' when he answered someone's call for help.

In his manuscript *Information*, Fr Rosario of Aliminusa declared: 'When I first arrived in San Giovanni Rotondo, I smelled it continually every day for three months, at the hour of Vespers. Whenever I left my cell, which was next to Padre Pio's, I would smell a strong, delightful fragrance which emanated from his room. I cannot exactly describe its characteristic. Once, on the first occasion, I smelled a strong, yet delicate perfume in the old sacristy; it was emanating from the chair that the Padre had used while hearing the men's confessions. Later, I passed in front of Padre Pio's cell and smelled a strong odour of carbolic acid. On other occasions, a light, delicate scent emanated from his hands.'

Fr Rosario of Aliminusa was the Guardian of the Friary of San Giovanni Rotondo from 18 September 1960 until 23 January 1964.

The persons who perceived Padre Pio's perfume during his lifetime, and since his death, are innumerable. We could continue writing the testimonies and declarations made by people who were the recipients of many favours, but we prefer to conclude by saying that Padre Pio's perfume was, and still is, a mysterious phenomenon which can appear strange and inexplicable, but which originates with that Supreme Giver of prodigies. Believers know that God's gifts surpass the imagination, and are sent in different forms at different times. They know that the gifts should be admired without question, and so they admire them with humility and veneration.

'Finally,' declares Miss Winowska, 'there is no doubt that this perfume has a very definite significance, that it is an addition to Padre Pio's apostolic arsenal; it is one more supernatural gift which God granted him for the purpose of helping, attracting, consoling, and warning souls that are entrusted to his care.'

Bilocation

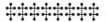

A mong the many charismatic gifts that our Lord gave his faithful servant, Padre Pio, was the gift of bilocation.

Although Catholic hagiography is rich in portentous phenomena, this is one of the rarest. Some of the saints who possessed this gift are: St Catherine of Ricci, St Anthony of Padua, and St Alphonsus de'Liguori. The latter was said to be in Sant'Agata dei Goti when he attended the dying Pope Clement XIV.

This supernatural phenomenon took place frequently with Padre Pio. Without leaving San Giovanni Rotondo, he presented himself and spoke to people who had never seen him before; therefore we can exclude the hypothesis of telepathy or hallucination.

He hurried to the bedside of the sick who had never met him physically, but who had invoked his help and intercession; and to the bedside of his spiritual children who sought his presence, his image, his paternal care.

From a letter written long ago, on 28 September 1915, by Padre Pio to one of his spiritual children, we begin to learn about the phenomenon of his bilocation.

'I am aware that this grace is truly important; the Lord chooses those whom He wants me to remember. Very often, in fact, our Lord presents people to me whom I have never seen, have never heard of, and asks me to pray for them; He then answers my every prayer. On the other hand, when the Lord does not wish to answer me, He makes me forget to pray for those persons even though I had the good and firm intention to do so.'

It's from Padre Pio himself that we learn how this phenomenon of bilocation takes place, through conversations with his fellow priests.

'One day in 1922,' wrote Fr Fernando of Riese Pio X, 'the friars of San Giovanni Rotondo were talking about the bilocation of St Anthony of Padua. It was close to his feast day. In answer to one friar's observation that perhaps these privileged sons of our Lord were not aware of their bilocation, Padre Pio, with the assurance of an expert on bilocation, answered: "Of course, they know. They might not know whether it's the body or the soul that moves, but they are fully aware of what is taking place, and where they are going."'

This answer confirms the fact that Padre Pio, with his characteristic simplicity, often described – in detail – places that he had never seen, or visited. In fact, in 1956, Fr Francesco Napolitano who had just returned from the United States, often spoke in the refectory about America, and especially about New York City. Padre Pio always enjoyed listening to him.

In answer to a strange question that the Padre asked, Fr Francesco said, 'Well, then, you have been to New York?'

And he replied, 'You've been there only once; I've been, hundreds of times.'

On another occasion Fr Francesco presented some pilgrims to him from Castellammare di Stabia, who wished to ask for his prayers. One lady of the group said, 'Father, I call on you, I invoke you every moment.'

'Yes!' replied Padre Pio; 'Do you think I am deaf? You have exasperated me with those little complaints of yours. It would be better if you had a little faith in God.'

Fr Rosario of Aliminusa, who was Padre Pio's Guardian for more than three years, wrote in his manuscript *Information* that there was an elderly lady in America who had an incurable tumour, and that her days were numbered. One day a friend of hers gave her a picture of Padre Pio and said, 'This friar can cure you.' The sick woman had never heard of the friar. One night he appeared before her, asked her to become a Catholic, and assured her that she would be cured. The sick woman called a Catholic priest; after a long period of instruction, she entered the Catholic Church. She was cured and lived a normal life.

This story became known even in San Giovanni Rotondo, and one day, Fr Eusebio of Castelpetroso, wanting to tease Padre Pio about it, said, 'So! You take an occasional trip to America! I found out that you went to see a lady who had a tumour.'

'How did you find out?' asked Padre Pio. And in reply to Fr Eusebio's question regarding the language he spoke when he travelled abroad, he said, 'Italian. How many miracles do you expect the Lord to perform!'

The fact that analogous deeds took place frequently with Padre Pio is confirmed by a series of irrefutable episodes. One such example is when Padre Pio was seen at the Vatican, kneeling and praying before the lamb of St Pius X, whom he always venerated. In Padre Pio's opinion, Pope Pius X was 'the most admirable of all the popes, since St Peter, because of his simplicity and humility, in which he resembled Jesus.'

Don Orione, now St Luigi Orione, said to Pope Pius XI that he had personally seen Padre Pio in the Basilica of St Peter in Rome during the beatification of Saint Thérèse of Lisieux. The pontiff, convinced, said to him, 'Since it is you who have said so, I believe it.'

Even the Bishop of Salto, Uruguay, Mgr Tomas Gregorio Camacho, mentioned the same episode, that the Padre was seen praying during the solemn ceremony. When a prelate drew near to speak to him, the friar of the Gargano disappeared.

It was perhaps after Don Orione's revelation that Rome adopted a more benevolent attitude towards Padre Pio, and relaxed the restrictions.

In Salto, Uruguay, we have the episode of Mgr Fernando Damiani, Vicar General of the Diocese, and one of Padre Pio's favourite souls. Don Fernando, during one of his frequent visits to Padre Pio, obtained the Padre's promise to assist him in the hour of death. The Padre kept that promise.

In 1941 the Archbishop of Montevideo, Mgr Antonio Maria Barbieri (later Cardinal), was invited to preside at the Eucharistic Congress which was held that year in Salto. One day, shortly after midnight, he was awakened by a knock at his bedroom door. In the shadows he thought he saw the form of a Capuchin priest. Then a voice said, 'Go help Mgr Damiani; he is dying.'

Archbishop Barbieri hurried to Mgr Damiani's bedside and had Fr Francesco Navarro administer the last rites. Mgr Damiani died a half hour later with four bishops and six priests in attendance.

On the nightstand they found the rough outline of a telegram which had been written by a trembling hand. It said, 'Padre Pio – San Giovanni Rotondo – repeated heart spasms are killing me – Damiani.'

Several years later, on 13 April 1949, Archbishop Barbieri went to San Giovanni Rotondo, and confirmed that the Capuchin he had seen in the shadows in Salto was Padre Pio.

While speaking of the Padre's bilocation, Cardinal Augusto Silj mentioned a child who had been declared incurable by the doctors. She was taken to San Giovanni Rotondo by her parents. They rented a room in a small hotel in town, put the child to bed, and went to the friary to solicit the Padre's prayers.

Unfortunately, that day Padre Pio was in bed, so it was impossible to approach him. Desolate, they turned back. When they arrived in town, their tears of sorrow turned to tears of joy, amazement, and gratitude to God: their child was running to meet them, jumping with joy.

'How did you manage to send me Padre Pio so quickly? He came and cured me.'

Another story is that of Fr Placido of San Marco in Lamis, a contemporary and classmate of Padre Pio. He became ill in July 1957 with hepatic cirrhosis, and was taken to the hospital of San Severo.

One day, around midnight, while Fr Placido was still awake, he saw Padre Pio approach his bed. He was smiling broadly and his hand was upraised. 'Placido,' he said, 'don't worry. You will not die!'

The next day the news became public knowledge in both the friary and the hospital. A few days later, the parish priest of Santa Maria delle Grazie in San Severo, Fr Alberto of San Giovanni Rotondo, met Padre Pio and asked him this question: 'Spiritual Father, have you been to San Severo lately?' 'Oh, yes,' he replied, 'but don't tell anyone about it.'

Fr Pio Dellepiane, a spiritual son of St Francis of Paola, was the confessor of Countess Virginia Silj, the sister-in-law of Cardinal Silj. He stated that one day the Countess wanted to bless and inaugurate a chapel in her apartment on Via del Tritone in Rome, and so sent out numerous invitations. Among those invited were her brother-in-law Cardinal Silj, who was at that time the Prefect of the Supreme Tribunal of the Apostolic Signature, and his cousin Cardinal Pietro Gasparri, Secretary of State of His Holiness.

While the Countess and the Church dignitaries were trying to decide to which saint the new chapel should be dedicated, a young nun arrived carrying a reliquary containing a relic of the Holy Cross.

The nun told everyone present that Padre Pio 'in the flesh' had come to her cell during the night, had given her the reliquary, and asked her to take it to Countess Silj the following morning.

The presence of the reliquary and the relic of the Holy Cross proved that it was not a dream. The two Cardinals confirmed the authenticity of the relic.

A few days later, the Countess went to San Giovanni Rotondo. Padre Pio assured her that the relic came from him, and that he had personally given it to the nun in Rome.

During the liberation of Italy towards the end of the Second World War, one of Padre Pio's spiritual daughters was arrested as a fascist, and condemned to death by a court martial. She was innocent of the charges, but how was she to prove it? The moment that they handcuffed her to lead her to the place of execution, she grabbed her rosary beads and a picture of Padre Pio.

'Padre,' she sobbed, 'help me!'

In transit, a delirious crowd insulted her and threw stones at her. More dead than alive, she finally reached the place where the firing squad awaited her. Suddenly, all traffic was completely stopped by long lines of armoured cars, ambulances, and troops that were travelling towards the North.

The head of the platoon ordered the execution to be deferred, then he stood up in the truck and waited as if he were hypnotised.

'As soon as they pass,' thought the young lady, 'my hour will come. Oh Padre, Padre, why aren't you here!'

Time passed, and the transport of troops continued. Exceedingly tired, and perhaps not so sure of themselves, the accusers dispersed. Only the commander of the platoon remained, standing as straight as an arrow, and as rigid as a sleepwalker.

Just as the last columns were about to pass on that fateful road, the noise of a motor startled the young lady.

An unknown gentleman arrived by car, declared point-blank that she was free, and kindly returned her to her home.

But the best part of the story is yet to come. In Italy, as in France, marauding bands plundered the houses of the condemned, grabbing the loot under the pretext of looking for explosives. At the very moment that a group of these thieves in disguise were about to break into the apartment of the condemned girl, right before the eyes of her terrified sister, an imperial and sonorous 'Stop!' made them come to a sudden halt.

They looked at one another, frightened, because the voice seemed to come from a powerful megaphone, of which they could find no trace. Another 'Stop!' which was angrier and more booming than the first, caused them to flee.

When the condemned girl returned home, her sister threw herself into her arms, sobbing, 'It was Padre Pio's voice! It was he who chased away the thieves!'

A few months later, when it became possible to travel again, the young lady took the train to San Giovanni Rotondo. Padre Pio greeted her with a smile, 'If you only knew how fast I had to travel because of your faith!' he said.

Finally, a case of bilocation which is unique in the history of saints, is one that took place during World War II. Padre

Pio's popularity grew rapidly towards the end of, and immediately after, the war. Soldiers of every nationality and religion – Europeans, Americans, Asians, Africans, and Oceanians – began to climb the Gargano mountain in order to meet the friar with the stigmata.

At this time, allied planes were ordered to bomb certain areas in Southern Italy, most of which was still under Nazi control. The city of Foggia had already been razed to the ground by aerial bombing. It was so bad that the friars, who were residents of the Provincial's friary of that city, took refuge in the Friary of San Giovanni Rotondo. San Giovanni Rotondo is about twenty miles in air distance from Foggia, and was close to being subjected to the same danger. However, while the allied bombers were flying over the Gargano, the pilots saw a friar in the air, with his arms raised, motioning to them not to release their bombs.

When the war ended, those fortunate aviators climbed the mountain of San Giovanni Rotondo, and to their amazement, they recognised Padre Pio as the friar whom they had seen in the air during their flights. Many of them became Catholics because of this extraordinary event, and ardently publicised the sanctity of the stigmatist.

From all this, we can very well say that our Lord gave His faithful servant many charismatic gifts, and that Padre Pio, who had a big and generous heart, placed them at everyone's disposal, especially the suffering and the sick.

Padre Pio's Sense of Humour

In the Friary of San Giovanni Rotondo, Padre Pio occupied cell No. 5 for more than twenty-five years. It was here that the most beautiful – and also the most painful – events in the life of this extraordinary man took place. Above his cell door are the words: 'The glory of the world is always accompanied by sadness.'

This maxim, taken from *The Imitation of Christ* was one that he applied to himself all his life; but for the glory of God, he also transformed – for himself and others – it to that other maxim, *Servite Domino in laetitia* ('Serve the Lord with joy').

He also adopted St Paul's words: 'Always be happy in the Lord; I repeat, be happy.' And the words of St Augustine: 'Sing and walk; sing with your voice, sing with your heart, sing with your deeds; and if the memory of yourself makes you sad, the thought of Him will fill you with joy.'

A special aspect of Padre Pio's joy was his sense of humour. His paternal guidance had a humorous, witty, brilliant, and vivacious side, and this played an important role in the education of his spiritual children. This side was most prevalent when he relaxed in the friary garden, or on the terrace near his cell. At those times he became an affectionate, cordial, happy, friendly Padre, even when those who were present were awed by his spiritual stature.

Most people think only of a Padre Pio who suffered, who obtained graces, and who constantly contemplated Christ crucified. They never knew Padre Pio in the intimacy of the friary, or in the warmth of the recreational hours which he spent daily with his fellow priests, friends, and spiritual children.

Considering his afflictions, this happy and humorous disposition of the Padre must not be interpreted as a dual personality. The Bible is very explicit in this respect: 'When you fast, do not have a gloomy aspect … when you fast, comb your hair and wash yourself.' The Padre wanted to teach all those who approached him to always have a smile on their lips.

Padre Pio was a joyful giver; he served God and served Him happily with a frank, innocent smile that stemmed from a pure heart. His spontaneity was admirable.

As the Jesuit, Fr Domenico Mondrone, wrote in the magazine, *Catholic Civilisation*, 'His expressions were pro- verbial. He would utter an amusing retort, a witty remark, a little joke, right in the middle of a conversation. Sometimes its purpose was to distract one's attention from his state of martyrdom; sometimes, to lighten the distressing effect of a well-aimed lesson.'

One day the Padre was out in the friary grounds, when the friar who was accompanying him pointed out a gentleman, a famous writer who had come from Milan for the sole purpose of seeing him. Padre Pio unhesitatingly responded, 'This long trip just to see me? What a fine thing you came to see, all the way from Milan! Don't you have a prayer book at home? You could have spared yourself a trip. God bless you. A Hail Mary is worth more than a trip, my son.'

Padre Pio was also a witty, brilliant, and formidable conversationalist. With psychological shrewdness, he would corner his listener, deliberately putting him in a difficult position. He could do this even when his opponent tried to involve him in scientific problems with which he was not familiar. At times he would disconcert them with seemingly bizarre remarks. Sometimes, he would stand up and mimic them, making them look ridiculous. He would suddenly change from the pathetic to the comical, or vice versa, depending on the effect he wished to have on his audience. Above all, his superabundance of humour escaped no one.

Once, in reply to someone who was trying to make him understand the difficulty some religious persons have in listening to, and practising the word of God, he said, 'Three things are useless: washing a donkey's head, adding water to the ocean, and preaching to sisters, friars and priests.'

Often, he teased the doctors of the hospital, who came every night to spend an hour of recreation with the Padre. One of them, when told to go to the hospital for some tests, said to his fellow director, 'What do we doctors know?' to which the director added 'But you, Father, have nevertheless built a hospital.' 'Yes, but only for sick people, not for doctors,' replied Padre Pio.

Small Joys
With filial confidence a devotee tries to remove the Padre's stole from his
shoulders. Pleased, he reacts with a smile.

One day, he said to a group of doctors, 'Don't forget the proverb of the Salerno School: "A mouse has a better chance with two cats than a sick person has with two doctors."'

He even joked about his own weakness. To a man who requested his prayers because his leg did not function properly, he quickly replied, 'You're lucky to have only one that doesn't function; I don't even have one that does!'

To a childless woman who wanted to know how to behave towards her nieces and nephews, he answered: 'Uncles and aunts are like chickens; the latter are plucked when they are dead, the former, while they are living.'

Soldiers and officers would often come to the Friary of San Giovanni Rotondo, especially after World War II. Once, when Padre Pio saw an officer who was looking rather sad, he approached him and said, 'Well, how come you're here today?' The officer explained that he had come to say goodbye because he was being transferred from Foggia to the north of Italy. Smiling at him, the Padre said, 'My son, these things happen only to friars and soldiers. You stay in one place, peacefully do your work, and just when you become accustomed to your environment, you are sent to the end of the world. Who knows why! But don't let it bother you; accept it and leave. Remember that it is your profession. The cassock and the uniform, believe me, are similar.'

Speaking of soldiers, he often liked to talk about his experience in the army in Naples. One rainy day in 1917, he was obliged to go to some place or another. Our soldier (Padre Pio) courageously armed himself with an umbrella; well sheltered, he took off for Piazza del Plebiscito.

'Hey, soldier!' But the soldier kept on going as if he hadn't heard a thing. 'Hey, by Jove, I'm talking to you, soldier.' It was a colonel, who had, naturally, become impatient. The Padre had to go back. 'What novelty is this?' yelled the colonel, while drowning in the downpour. 'A soldier with an umbrella! Are you crazy?'

'I had to play stupid,' said Padre Pio with a sly smile. 'I offered him my umbrella: "If the colonel, sir, wishes to share my umbrella, I will accompany him." The colonel understood that he was dealing with a dumb recruit, so with a spiteful gesture, he turned his back to me, leaving me standing there with my umbrella in hand.'

There are other military stories that Padre Pio told with a good deal of pleasure; the one about the military simpletons being instructed by sergeants, and the one about the infantryman who was being prepared for the imminent visit of the King. (Italy was a Kingdom at that time.) The sergeant in charge of preparing the soldier knew that the conversation between the King and the recruit never varied. It usually took this form:

1. Question: 'How old are you?'
   Answer: 'Twenty-two.'
2. Question: 'How many years of service do you have?'
   Answer: 'Two.'
3. Question: 'Which do you serve more willingly, your King or your country?'
   Answer: 'Either one or the other.'

The sergeant patiently trained the private along these guidelines, and after much effort, he succeeded in learning it by heart.

Finally the King arrived. He reviewed the troops, and as was foreseen, asked questions. The questions were the same, but the order was reversed.

1. Question: 'How many years of service do you have?'
   Answer: 'Twenty-two.'
2. Question: 'How old are you?'
   Answer: 'Two.'

The sergeant broke out in a cold sweat, and the King impatiently exclaimed: 'Either you're a fool, or I am!'

The soldier, who knew the lesson by heart, gave the third reply: 'Either one or the other, your Majesty.'

At those times the Padre had a childlike simplicity in spite of his age; his laughter burst forth from his innocent heart.

Whenever Padre Pio told the joke about the drunkard, he always got up from his chair and acted out the part. 'Why, oh Lord,' said the drunkard, who had seen a centipede walking on the wall, 'did you give this little animal a hundred legs, and to me who cannot stand up straight, only two?'

'If anyone interrupted him, spoiling the effect of the story, which he told with fantastic ease,' wrote Lorenzo Bedeschi, 'he was not annoyed. He would accept the interruption and make a joke of it with one of his usual remarks, "Oh, this half-wit!"'

'We exchanged many witty remarks during our political discussions,' said Bedeschi. 'I, naturally, in order to get him to open up, would side with the government. But his humour always prevented me from imposing any serious problems.

'The bell rang out the Ave Maria. It was the end of the recreational hour. Padre Pio stood up and recited the Angelus. He no sooner finished the prayer than he resumed the interrupted discussion which regarded the omission of God's name from the Constitutional Charter of the Republic. He said in an imperious voice, "Social offenses are not like individual offenses which can be expiated here below. God does not tolerate nations which refuse to recognise Him, and refuse to include Him." Then, turning to me, he said, "I got you there, young fellow!"'

Generally he wouldn't tell stories just for the sake of talking, but utilised his recreational time to tell little jokes that were instructional, that contained a moral, or were religious.

The Madonna, who was Padre Pio's great love, also had a place in his little anecdotes.

'One day,' he said, 'the Lord took a walk through Paradise and saw so many ugly faces wandering around this place that is so full of delightful things and so void of evil. The Lord was amazed, so He sent for St Peter and asked him, "Peter, what has happened? It seems as if we have transferred the jail to Paradise." Peter replied, "Lord, I don't know; they come in and I don't know how they enter." The Lord then ordered him to guard more carefully.

'Once more the Lord took a walk through Paradise, and again He saw an increase of ugly faces – jailbirds, so He said to St Peter, "Peter I told you to be on guard. Give me the keys; you are no longer guarding well."

'Peter replied, "Lord, I didn't want to tell you, but since you insist, I will tell you. I no sooner turn my back than Your Mother opens the door and lets them all come in. I'm helpless. Lord, how do You feel about it? What must I do when Your Mother goes to the door?"

'The Lord answered, "Peter, just pretend you don't see it."'

The conclusion is eloquent in the sense that the Virgin Mary is always everyone's mother, and without her, Paradise would not be the same.

Padre Pio's wit was part of his apostolate. He sometimes used it to confuse a soul, or to better penetrate the secrets of the conscience.

In this manner some people were able to review some aspect of their lives; while others, feeling exposed, overhauled their lives and became true friends of Christ, and therefore, of Padre Pio.

Every hour of the day was an opportune time to ask Padre Pio's advice, including the hours of rest in the afternoon. Often, his fellow priests would come in because some penitent had sent them.

Once a woman went to the porter, and with a certain amount of insistence, convinced him that he should go to Padre Pio's cell to ask his advice regarding her health. The young friar, in the spirit of brotherly love, tried to please her, so he went and knocked on the door of the Padre's cell. A voice answered, 'What do you want? Can't you see that I am resting?'

'Spiritual Father,' said the friar, 'a lady from Genoa who is very sick wants to know whether she should continue or discontinue the electroshocks.'

Padre Pio, minimising the importance of the reply, retorted, 'But I'm resting! Tell her to discontinue, because if she isn't already a fool, she will certainly become one.'

Padre Pio's life of mysticism, observed Spaccucci, did not lessen in the least his natural tendency to playful banter, to scholarly language, and to impart his happiness in a spiritual way to all those who were present.

For example, the comedian Carlo Campanini went to Padre Pio and said, 'Father, how can I boast of being a member of your spiritual family when every night I have to paint my face and be a buffoon on the stage?'

Padre Pio smiled, 'My son, in this world everyone is a buffoon no matter where God places him. It is sufficient to surmise what God wants, and then everything will take its proper place. There once was an acrobat who wanted to become a friar, but since he was very ignorant he didn't succeed in learning the hymns and prayers, unlike his fellow friars. So when the church was empty, the acrobat would go before the statue of the Madonna and exhibit his only talent: somersaults and pirouettes.

'When it was found out, it became the great scandal of the friary. One morning the Guardian hid behind a column hoping to take the acrobat by surprise. Imagine the Guardian's surprise when he saw the statue of the Holy Virgin smile, and the statue of the Child Jesus clap hands; both were so pleased with the performance of the acrobat in the grey cassock!

'So the most ignorant friar of the community offered the Queen of Heaven his only talent, and she accepted it with joy. That friar had chosen his position well. He was a good buffoon in the place that God had assigned to him.'

Thus Padre Pio's humour, Fr Alessandro wrote, became apostolic; it was not just a pastime. His holy soul was never shocked by sin, but he always found a way to put everything in its proper place.

Padre Pio's sense of humour, his witticism, his repartee, were not just for amusement and spiritual defence, but were also a defence against the curious and the annoying.

Between a smile and a joke he hid his secret, so that many of those who lived near him never suspected a thing; some never even understood his goodness and his heroic virtues. He said the most serious of things with such simplicity and sincerity, that he made you accept the supernatural without even noticing it. He was always between two lives, smiling and exchanging words with the beings of two worlds.

We can safely say that in that hour of recreation, the friary garden, the terrace, and his cell were transformed into a place of human activity, of spiritual equality, of brotherly love and perfect happiness.

While the spiritual children of this Stigmatist of the Gargano are still alive, asserts Spaccucci, society will learn to accept what he taught with his blood. His name will be uttered with warmth, and it will be understood, once and for all, why he was loved by so many people.

Padre Pio is no longer physically with us, but his spirit is still calling numerous people to his tomb to testify that his life and works were in harmony with the plans of Providence.

Padre Pio and the Madonna

'The picture of Padre Pio,' wrote Fr Fernando of Riese Pio X, 'would be incomplete if we did not emphasise, as he did during his life, his devotion to the Madonna. During the eight decades of his life, the image of the Madonna appears, like a filigree, during his most difficult moments.

'The love that was born at the dawn of his life in Pietrelcina, shone brightly until the earthly sunset of Padre Pio in San Giovanni Rotondo. So much of the secret of Padre Pio was clarified by the Madonna who was, during his childhood, a reassuring Mother, and in the darkest hours of his life, his ally in battle.

'The newborn Francesco Forgione opened his eyes to Christianity when he was baptised in the Church of St Anne in Pietrelcina, called Santa Maria degli Angeli; the octogenarian, Padre Pio, closed his eyes just a few metres from the church of San Giovanni Rotondo which is called Santa Maria delle Grazie. A distinctly Marian coverage!'

Padre Pio nurtured his love for the Mother of Jesus from the time he was a child. He would go to the church in Pietrelcina to greet and to pray to the Our Lady of Graces.

He always kept a little picture of this Madonna hanging on the wall of his little cell. He would glance up at her with gratitude before eating his meager meals, before going to rest, and each time he returned to his cell weary and fatigued after hearing confessions. He was to look up at his little Mother with immense tenderness before closing his eyes in death.

Padre Pio's love for the Madonna was that of a friend who has faith, who believes and hopes. It was not just sentimental piety expressed in beautiful phrases, sighs and sobs! His love for the Mother of God was the result of constant meditation which had become his way of life.

Padre Pio contemplated Mary within God's plan for the salvation of mankind. By being close to her, he felt closer to Jesus.

On 6 May 1913, Padre Pio wrote to Fr Agostino of San Marco in Lamis: 'This most tender Mother in her great mercy, wisdom, and goodness, has punished me in a most exalted manner, by pouring so many great graces into my heart that when I am in her presence, or that of Jesus, I am compelled to exclaim, Where am I? Who is near me? I am all aflame. I feel myself held fast and bound to the Son by means of His Mother.'

His love became an endless, ardent, faithful prayer. Who could possibly count the rosaries that he recited over the course of his marvelous life? He was the Friar of the Rosary. He always carried it in his hand or on his arm as if it were a bracelet or a shield. He had other rosaries under the pillow of his bed, on the bureau in his cell. He called the rosary his 'weapon'. One night when he was sick in bed, he was unable to find his rosary beads, so he called Fr Onorato of San Giovanni Rotondo, saying, 'Young man, get me my weapon; give me my weapon.'

The rosary was his favourite prayer; he recited it continually. He devoured the rosary with insatiable hunger. It was the prayer that he had learned from the Virgin, herself, the Virgin of Pompeii, Lourdes, and Fatima, as a means of obtaining the conversion and salvation of sinners.

At certain hours, he would walk down the centre path of the friary garden, absorbed in his suffering and in his love, while the beads slipped through the fingers of his wounded hands. In his pockets he carried rosary beads which he would give to anyone who requested one. Even today, people still hold these dear, saying 'This is a rosary which Padre Pio gave me; I treasure it with all my heart!'

When the friary bell rang and he was able to recite the Angelus, either in the garden, or in church, or at his window, how passionate his voice was! Standing at the altar, reading the 'Visit to Mary Most Holy', he was rarely able to control his emotions. He was deeply moved when Beniamino Gigli sang Gounod's Ave Maria for him in the friary garden.

He had a weakness for these famous singers; he listened to them with such pleasure, and always requested them to sing either a prayer to the Madonna, or a Neapolitan song. He was so attentive, and so fascinated, that it was as though he was enjoying a bit of Paradise.

Fr Francesco Napolitano relates that one day, after the

evening services, Padre Pio quickly took off his stole and surplice, and though the sacristy was full of men, he ignored them all and ran towards the choir: the famous tenor Damiani had come from Montevideo to see him, and was going to sing 'Oh, Madre di Pietà' written by Fr Ludovico of San Marco in Lamis.

One night, he heard a group of pilgrims singing a Marian song under his window: 'You are as beautiful as the sun, as white as the moon.'

He commented: 'If that were so, I'd refuse to go to Paradise.'

Indeed, there were many times he would get up in the wee hours of the night to open the window of his cell because someone outside, alone, was singing either Shubert's Ave Maria, or Gounod's Ave Maria in his honour. He would be enraptured, and at the end he would applaud and shout, 'Bravo, bravo ... may the Madonna protect and bless you, my son.'

In 1959, the pilgrim statue of Our Lady of Fatima was leaving Cova da Iria, Portugal, in a helicopter to tour the major provinces of Italy, and Padre Pio awaited the coming of the statue of his beloved Madonna. However, at the time the Padre was suffering from a serious case of pleurisy, which lasted quite some time and prevented his celebrating Mass since the fifth of May. His inability to celebrate Mass and to hear confessions caused him so much suffering that he anxiously awaited the arrival of Our Lady of Fatima.

Every night, from 31 March, he would utter a spiritual thought into a microphone, which was connected to the loudspeaker. Thus, he could be heard by all the faithful who were gathered in the church. On the evening of 4 August he announced: 'We have but a few hours for our Mother's visit. Let us not be found empty-handed!' On the evening of 4 August, he announced with a voice full of emotion: 'In a few minutes our Mother will be in our home … Let us open our hearts.'

On the morning of 6 August, throngs of people were in the church. The Padre, too, attended, accompanied by his fellow priests. Exhausted, he had to sit down, and remained a long time in front of the image of the Madonna. When the little statue was placed before him for him to kiss, he placed in her hands the rosary that had been a gift from the Prayer Group of San Casciano in Val di Pesa. That affectionate and touching gesture brought tears to the eyes of all who were present.

When, at last, the helicopter rose from the terrace of the Home for the Relief of Suffering, among the eyes that followed it were his, wet with tears … He called her by name: 'Beautiful little Mother, I have been sick during your visit to Italy; now you are leaving without curing me!'

He would have preferred to die rather than remain unable to celebrate Mass and hear confessions. But the moment he lamented her departure, Padre Pio felt a chill through his body. He exclaimed to his fellow priests: 'I am cured!'

And so he was. This became known to everyone. Fr Francesco Neopolitano, who had been present at that scene, said that Padre Pio never felt so healthy and strong as he did after the departure of the statue of Our Lady of Fatima.

Certain insinuations of the press were addressed when Padre Pio, with his usual childlike simplicity, said to his spiritual director Fr Agostino of San Marco in Lamis, 'The Madonna came because she wanted to cure Padre Pio!'

For the Stigmatist of the Gargano, love for the Madonna meant perpetual imitation of her. If Jesus is the way and the light which leads to the Father, Mary is the way and the light which leads to Jesus. With Mary's help, and by imitating her virtues, Padre Pio drew ever closer to Jesus, so very close as to be transformed into Him.

The Madonna
Padre Pio's love for the Madonna became an endless, ardent, faithful prayer.
He was the Friar of the Rosary.

His imitation of Mary meant, most importantly, imitation of her humility. For him that humility was a constant interior torment, a slow and painful agony, the anguish of not knowing whether he was corresponding to divine grace. You could read that deep humility on his face even when he was surrounded by clamorous crowds who believed in him, who trusted in his prayers and expected so many miracles from him every day. He always remained collected. His humility made it possible for him to be serene and dignified as he silently accepted mortification, slander, quarrels, humiliation, and sorrow.

For him, love of the Madonna signified perpetual mortification. He implored his spiritual director to allow him to make a vow of abstinence from fruit on Wednesdays; he also asked him to suggest a means of pleasing the Blessed Mother in all things at all times.

Love of the Madonna animated him, and inspired him all the more to become an apostle. 'I should like to have a voice strong enough to invite all the sinners of the world to love the Madonna.' God heard this sigh of love: he was given a voice that could be heard even when he was silent. It was a voice that touched the depths of people's hearts, that penetrated their consciences, that tormented and shook those who were dormant. It was a voice that was as terrible as the crashing of thunder in the night, yet as sweet as a caress. It was a voice that was threatening, yet inviting; a voice that annihilated yet restored, that consoled and pardoned.

To all those who recommended themselves to his prayers, Padre Pio would say: 'Love the Madonna. Recite the rosary.'

One day, his Guardian asked him how many rosaries he recited daily. Padre Pio answered, 'Well, I have to tell my Guardian the truth; I have recited thirty-four!' For him the rosary was a perpetual meditation on the profound mysteries of Calvary, on Jesus' plan of salvation, on His sorrowful Mother. Padre Pio was fascinated by the Hail Mary.

Padre Pio was deeply devoted to Our Lady of Pompeii. He never failed to pay her a visit whenever he had the opportunity to go to Pompeii. He went to this mystical sanctuary for the first time in 1901, when he was fourteen years old, accompanied by his teacher and seven schoolmates. As a soldier, during his military service at Naples, he never failed to run down to Pompeii from time to time, to say 'hello' to his 'beautiful Virgin'.

A few days before his death, on the eve of the fiftieth anniversary of his stigmata, he was offered a bouquet of roses. He was deeply touched, and with a slight gesture towards his picture of the Virgin Mother, he took a rose and asked one of his spiritual children to take it to Pompeii and place it in front of the image of the Madonna.

'That rose,' wrote Fr Gerardo Di Flumeri, 'did not wilt; it remained beautiful, fresh, and fragrant until the day of the Padre's death, then it closed and became a bud again.'

That rose is the symbol of the venerated Padre's love for the 'beautiful Virgin', his beloved 'Mother of Pompeii'.

The Last Anniversary of the Stigmata

Everyone was talking about Padre Pio, and people were arriving from all parts of the world. Life in the friary proceeded as usual, and while the Padre intensified his prayers, everyone else was preparing to commemorate and celebrate the fiftieth anniversary of his stigmata. There was nothing to indicate that his end was near.

The community leaders of San Giovanni Rotondo planned great festivities for 20 September 1968. The director of the Prayer Groups announced to all the members that Sunday, the 22nd, there would be an international convention held there. Many other commemorative activities were planned in Padre Pio's honour.

The 20th of September was a glorious, radiant day. The people participated en masse in the festivities planned by the town council. Everyone was deeply touched and filled with gratitude.

The following notation is found in the chronicles of the friary: 'There was nothing impressive except the many, many red roses decorating the main altar; they had been given to him by his spiritual children. A great multitude of spiritual children had come from all over the world to be with the Padre on this memorable day.'

Fifty years previous, Padre Pio had been there, in the choir, enjoying a peaceful, uninterrupted calm, when suddenly a mysterious 'person' dripping with blood appeared. When that 'person' disappeared, Padre Pio noticed that his hands, feet, and side, were stained with blood.

Fifty years later, 20 September 1968, the old choir seemed to echo the events of that Friday full of visions and blood.

Some vases of flowers were placed on the wooden railing at the sides of the crucifix. Baskets of roses were in front of the picture of Our Lady of Grace in the apse of the little church. This was the only sign of homage, the only commemoration of this most unusual fiftieth anniversary that existed in the old choir, in the little church sanctified by Padre Pio's presence over the long years.

More than two thousand people crowded the church in order to hear Padre Pio's Mass. It took about a quarter of an hour, according to Trombetta, for everyone to enter when the bronze doors were opened. The patient crowd had waited in the square under the stars, through the windy night, while the lights of the stars shone brightly, and shadows gradually made their way to the friary, arriving from every street.

At one minute to five, Padre Pio climbed the steps to the altar and, seated in his chair, he began the old but ever new dialogue with God.

It was a Mass without hymns, without liturgical activity, without Communion for the faithful, without a homily, without community prayers. Only the quavering voice of Padre Pio animated the length and breadth of the church.

As if nailed to the altar, his every need anticipated by his fellow priests at all times, the Padre solemnly celebrated the Mass of the fiftieth anniversary of his stigmata.

Gusts of fresh air blew through the open doors, but the church was steaming with the heat of the bodies, and the breath of all those beings gathered in prayer with Padre Pio.

The legions of souls whom he had favoured were all spiritually present at Padre Pio's fiftieth anniversary Mass. The border of red roses along the balustrades of the church was a symbol of their presence and gratitude.

At five-thirty, the Padre finished the Mass, then remained praying for a few minutes, before his fellow priests helped him to get up. He was practically carried away, bent over with pain; a living picture of a crucified man. Fortunately, the crowd neither shouted nor applauded as they had on other occasions of his life.

Thus, this exceptional fiftieth anniversary passed without clamour, and without any real signs of festivity. The church was constantly filled with priests who were celebrating Mass. Nuns and priests from all of Italy and from abroad had come. Fellow priests from the entire religious province had wanted to be near him for the jubilee of his pain and blood.

The day ended with a tremendous candlelight procession in which the entire population of San Giovanni Rotondo, and all the pilgrims, took part. The procession wound its way from the village to the friary of the Capuchins at about ten o'clock at night. It was a sea of light as a Biblical-type crowd climbed the friary road – a road that was once a rough path excavated on the side of a barren, deserted mountain. Today it is crowded with houses, hotels, restaurants, stores, stalls, cars, and lights.

The city of San Giovanni Rotondo, its Mayor, Dr Giuseppe Sala, and the entire administration of the community, wanted to commemorate this fiftieth anniversary which was unique in the history of the saints, and of the Church. It was truly an impressive spectacle, the sea of lights undulating, moving, advancing as the band played. The church square overflowed, and they gathered under the open window of the old choir, waiting to see their Padre, to thank him and shout, 'Viva, Padre Pio!'

Later, the crowd moved behind the cloister wall directly under the window of Padre Pio's cell, and waited at length for the Padre to open the window and give them the blessing that they so desired. Alas, they waited in vain!

Padre Pio was lying on his little bed, suffering more than ever before. It was late, and Padre Pio had been resting for about two hours; he never saw, never heard, never noticed anything. He hadn't the faintest notion that all the festivities were in his honour.

The day ended with an artistic and lengthy display of fireworks. Nothing disturbed Padre Pio's tranquility – not the noise, the applause, nor the shouting. The following morning he asked his fellow priests, 'What was all that noise last night?'

'On 21 September,' according to Fr Alessandro of Ripabottoni, 'Padre Pio did not celebrate Mass, but only received Communion, because of his weakness and loss of strength resulting from a severe attack of asthma which impeded his breathing and aroused fear and apprehension. He was attended by Dr Giuseppe Sala and all his fellow priests who didn't move from Padre Pio's room until the crisis was over and he was feeling better.'

The following is written in the chronicles of the friary: 'Padre Pio, however, was in deep pain and very upset. He kept holding the hands of the Guardian and of those fellow priests who were standing near him. The doctors and everyone kept admonishing him to be brave, that it would soon be over, as it always was. The Padre kept looking at everyone around him, repeating: "It's the end! It's the end!"'

In the afternoon, as usual, he attended Vespers from the balcony, and blessed the large crowd which had come from all parts of the world to attend the International Convention of the Prayer Groups, which was to be held the next day.

Padre Pio's Last Mass

The International Convention of Prayer Groups brought an enormous crowd to San Giovanni Rotondo, one that was to be surpassed only by the crowd that rushed to the friary upon hearing of Padre Pio's death.

Everything was ready for the celebration; the Home for the Relief of Suffering was decorated with lights and waving banners, and the church of the friary was adorned like a beautiful bride. The hotels were filled to capacity, reservations made three months in advance. Many people sought rooms in the nearby cities and towns, while others waited either outside or in a bus for that glorious and memorable day to dawn.

'Everyone was celebrating,' wrote the chronicler of the friary, burning with anxious desire for the next day to dawn. Only Padre Pio, with his usual humility, was confused and bewildered, in contemplation of the great gifts that God had given him.

'What a celebration!' the Padre said to his Guardian, 'I am so confused that I should like to run and hide.'

The faithful and diligent chroniclers have noted that, in the history of the Friary of San Giovanni Rotondo, no single day can compare to the one experienced on 22 September 1968. This historic event, the International Convention of Prayer Groups, will linger in the memory of all who were present.

At five o'clock, Padre Pio wanted to celebrate his usual Low Mass, but the Guardian gently insisted that he celebrate a Solemn High Mass for the Convention of Prayer Groups. Padre Pio obeyed.

As soon as the church doors opened, the people literally swarmed to the aisles and the pews; every inch of space was occupied, leaving many people out in the square.

Padre Pio, assisted by Fr Pellegrino of Sant'Elia a Pianisi, walked slowly and wearily to the sacristy, and after the usual preparations, he put on his sacred vestments. Then, accompanied by Frs Onorato and Valentino of San Giovanni Rotondo (deacon and subdeacon respectively), he walked to the altar to celebrate Holy Mass. The crowd went wild with the joy of seeing him and honouring him; it took considerable effort to obtain silence and order.

No one, however, suspected that this was to be his last Mass. The balustrade of the church was still adorned with red roses. Red flowers were everywhere. No one could know that they involuntarily symbolised the final sacrifice of the man of God whose life had been spent for the good of souls, in his ardent love for God. It was a Mass of agony. When he raised the Sacred Host and chalice he stared at them as if he were seeing in them the unfathomable mystery of the Invisible. His eyes were glassy; they could no longer perceive human things.

The Last Mass
Padre Pio celebrated his last Holy Mass in the early morning of 22 September
1968, the day before his death. He sang a solemn High Mass for the Prayer
Groups which had gathered for a convention.

'The Mass', according to the chronicles of the friary,
'proceeded with its usual solemnity. At the end, with
thunderous and interminable applause and sincere cries of
Viva Padre Pio – "Best Wishes Padre!", they took leave of the
Padre before he returned to the sacristy. However, upon
getting up from his chair and going down the steps of the
altar which faced the people, Padre Pio staggered, bent over,
and almost fell. His assistants, especially Br Bill, promptly
grabbed him, held him up, eased him into his wheel chair,
and accompanied him to the sacristy.

'The Padre, who was very pale, leaned on the side railing, and in a rather absent and bewildered manner blessed the crowd, repeating breathlessly and affectionately, 'My children, my children.' After his thanksgiving, he went towards the women's confessional, passing through a crowd of men and priests, but he had to turn back and take the elevator to his room. Padre Pio no longer seemed like himself; weak and pale, his hands cold, he stared at everyone with a faraway look, unaware of what was going on around him. And that is the way he remained the entire day.'

At around ten-thirty, he succeeded in going to the window of the old church choir, where fifty years previously he had received the stigmata. He blessed and greeted the Prayer Groups who were gathered on the square. Fr Onorato, seeing that he was worn out, tried to dissuade him. But Padre Pio won; even though his body was broken, his heart was overflowing with love. 'I want to greet my children for the last time.'

It is difficult to describe the joy, the excitement, the hand clapping, the shouts of 'Viva', the waving of hands and white handkerchiefs, in response to the Padre's greeting. That stupendous crowd, which had come from far and wide, demonstrated their filial love and devotion to him once more.

It was a moment of sheer joy, of energy and passion; then the Padre, with help, retired to his room.

He kept the last appointment of the day, that evening. He wanted to attend the evening Mass for the Prayer Groups.

When the Mass ended, he tried to get up to bless the crowd, but remained bent over, unable to move. He was barely able to raise his right hand to bless his spiritual children. His fellow priests held him, placed him in the wheelchair and accompanied him to his cell. Passing through the vestibule of St Francis, he greeted and blessed many men and women, and from the window of his cell he greeted and blessed the crowd, waving a white handkerchief.

After repeated salutations and cries of 'Viva! Best Wishes! Goodnight, Padre! We love you so much, Padre!' the window of Padre Pio's cell was closed forever, shutting behind it the vision and memory of a man whom everyone called 'father'.

Serene Transition

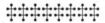

Who would have imagined that the festivities of the previous day were to be followed by a funeral the next day?

Everyone could see that Padre Pio was slowly failing, and he himself often spoke of his desire to die: 'Only the tomb is missing. I belong more to the other world than to this. Pray to our Lord that I may die!'

One may read in the chronicles of the friary: 'He wanted to die while still actively at work, spending the day, as usual, in prayer and in the administration of his ministerial duties for the good of souls. He certainly appeared to be unusually weary, as if he were in another world. Some people say that he was meant to die on the altar when he staggered at the end of the Mass, and that our Lord kept him alive a while longer in order not to spoil the festivities of the day, in order not to cause any inconveniences. But who would have suspected that the end was so close?'

At about two o'clock in the morning, a friar was knocking on the door of the Guardian's cell: 'Guardian, please get up. Padre Pio is very sick.'

The Guardian, Fr Carmelo of San Giovanni in Galdo, said: 'I hurried to Padre Pio's room and found Fr Pellegrino,

Br Bill and Dr Sala with the Padre who was sitting up in a chair. The Padre's eyes were closed, his head was slightly bent, and he was breathing heavily; there was a slight rattle in his throat. I took his right hand; it was already cold. I called him several times, Padre, Padre! He didn't answer me.'

In the meantime, Fr Paolo of San Giovanni Rotondo administered the Sacrament of the Sick to the Padre, while Fr Raffaele of Sant'Elia a Pianisi (the last confessor and Superior of the Padre for many years) and Fr Mariano of Santa Croce di Magliano were kneeling, responding to the prayers.

In the meantime, the Padre was given oxygen and artificial respiration. The friars recited the prayers for a dying soul. Padre Pio was calm and serene; he was no longer breathing. His head had bent slightly towards his chest. Dr Sala stopped feeling his pulse and said sadly, 'He's gone!' It was two-thirty in the morning, Monday, 23 September 1968.

Padre Pio did not want to die in bed. He died seated in his modest armchair where he had spent hour after hour in prayer, in meditation, and in preparation for Holy Mass; the armchair from which he had listened to, advised, enlightened and comforted so many fellow priests, spiritual children, anguished souls, bishops and others who had the good fortune of seeing him in his cell.

There, in his place of work, with his rosary in hand, and wearing his religious habit, he awaited the coming of the Lord.

Fr Pellegrino, who had the good fortune of being with him until the end, gives us some edifying details of that last night.

'Padre Pio, by means of the intercom, called me to his cell. He was in bed lying on his right side. He only asked me to look at the clock on the bureau and tell him the time. I dried the tears that were gleaming in his reddened eyes, and returned to room No. 4 to listen to the intercom which was always turned on.

'The Padre called me about five or six times up until midnight. His eyes were always red from crying, but he cried quietly, serenely.

'At midnight, like a frightened child, he begged me: "Stay with me, my son," and began to ask me the time more frequently. He looked at me with imploring eyes, and held my hands tightly.

'Then, as if he had forgotten the time, which he had continually asked me for, he said, "My son, have you said Mass yet?"

'I smiled and replied, "Spiritual Father, it's too early for Mass." He answered, "Well, this morning you will say it for me."

'Immediately, he wanted to make his confession. After confession he said, "My son, if the Lord calls me today, ask all my brothers to forgive me for all the trouble I have caused them: and ask all our fellow priests and my spiritual children to say a prayer for my soul."

'I replied, "Spiritual Father, I am sure that the Lord will let you live for a long time yet, but just in case you should be right, may I ask you to give your last blessing to your fellow priests, your spiritual children, and your patients?"

'He answered, "Of course, I bless them all! Ask the Guardian to give all of them this last blessing from me."

'Finally, he said he wanted to renew his religious vows.

'It was about one o'clock when he said, "Listen, my son; I can't breathe well here in bed. Let me get up. I will be able to breathe better sitting up in the chair."

'One o'clock, two o'clock, three o'clock – these were the hours when he usually got up to prepare himself for the celebration of Holy Mass, and before sitting in the armchair, he used to take a little walk down the corridor. That night, much to my surprise, he walked straight and lively, like a young man, so much so, that I did not have to hold him up. At the door of his cell, he said, "Let's go to the terrace for a little while." I followed him, and held his arm. He, himself, turned on the light, and going straight to the armchair, sat down and looked about him curiously. He seemed to be looking for something. After five minutes he asked to return to his cell.

'Back in the cell, I noticed that the Padre was beginning to grow pale. He was sweating cold. I became alarmed when I noticed that his lips were turning dark blue. He kept repeating, in a voice that grew weaker and weaker, "Jesus, Mary." I started for the door to call a fellow priest, but he stopped me and said, "Don't awaken anyone." I implored him, "Spiritual Father, please let me go."'

Death – Sorrow – Tears

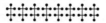

All those who were present when he passed away kissed his hand and said a prayer for the deceased Padre. Then, the Guardian asked everyone to leave the room so that Padre Pio's body could be prepared according to custom. Only he, Fr Raffaele, Fr Mariano, and Dr Sala remained.

The stigmata were examined, and Fr Giacomo of Montemarano photographed them for the official records.

The Guardian of that time, Fr Carmelo of San Giovanni in Galdo wrote: 'I knew that I had to leave an official and authoritative testimony, so immediately, in the presence of witnesses, I closely examined the stigmata and found that his hands were no longer the same. The wounds of his hands, feet, and side had completely healed without even the slightest trace of a scar.

'There were two mysterious aspects: the absence of the stigmata, and the absence of any sign or trace or a scar. Nevertheless, no one can doubt that Padre Pio had the stigmata while alive; everyone saw them, and thousands of photographs were taken of them. As a matter of fact, the last scab became detached from his left hand at the time of his death.'

Dr Giuseppe Sala made the following declaration: 'In conclusion, the palm and the back of his hands, the backs and soles of his feet, and the left side of his chest had normal, unbroken skin, uniform in colour exactly like the remainder of his body which was pale and motionless due to his recent death.'

The existence of Padre Pio's wounds during his lifetime, and their disappearance at his death, is not to be considered a medical phenomenon, but rather, a supernatural phenomenon.

As a personal opinion, the Guardian, in contemplating this phenomenon, advanced the following theory:

1. It is possible that Padre Pio, himself, asked the Lord to hide the visible gifts when he died. During his lifetime he did everything possible to hide his wounds which embarrassed and humiliated him because of their uniqueness; he would not have been able to do this after his death. The Lord may have answered his prayers and made the wounds completely disappear like any wound that heals over time.

2. Padre Pio may have received the stigmata from the Lord, not for the purpose of showing them to others, but for himself. In this sense they were a personal thing, his participation in the horrible suffering and passion of Christ Crucified. By uniting himself with the suffering Christ, Padre Pio offered himself for the salvation of many souls.

As such, with his death, there was no further need for the stigmata. The victim had been drained in fifty years, and no longer had a drop of blood to give.

This hypothesis, however, does not explain the absence of scars.

3. There is another hypothesis, though it might seem rather bold. All saints suffer a period of spiritual aridity, to the point where they no longer feel Divine comfort and consider themselves doomed. Even Jesus on the Cross cried, 'My God, my God, why have you forsaken me?'

Couldn't this have been the last great trial to which God subjected Padre Pio's soul; to have him die on Calvary, like Jesus? This trial would have begun with the gradual disappearance of the stigmata, two or three months before his death, or even sooner. Many people claimed that the external signs of Padre Pio's wounds were beginning to disappear. This would have ended with their complete disappearance at his death, causing Padre Pio the greatest torment of his life – the loss of God's gift.

As soon as the examination of the stigmata was over, his body was prepared and taken to the veranda near his room; this became the mortuary until he was laid out in church.

Padre Pio was beautiful and solemn even in death, wearing his stole and holding a crucifix, a rosary, and the Franciscan Rule in his hands.

The sad news spread through the world in a flash, to shock, sorrow, and tears. To give some idea of how fast the painful news travelled, the following message was broadcast on Radio Rome (a news report for Italians abroad) in Chile, half an hour after the Padre's death: 'We have just learned this moment, that the Stigmatist of the Gargano, Padre Pio of Pietrelcina, died in San Giovanni Rotondo, Province of Foggia. In our next bulletin we will give the latest details.'

In Pietrelcina, the native town of the deceased, the church bells sounded a brief funeral toll, then pealed festively every half hour.

People from Italy and abroad hurried to the Capuchin Friary of the Gargano. Truckloads of Carabinieri were already stationed in the church square and at all strategic points, including the gate of the little court where the grotto of Lourdes is, and at the iron gate of the garden.

Inside the church, preparations were being made for the public to view the body. An enormous crowd already blocked the entrance to the closed church. People embraced each other and cried. The workmen prepared a passage to direct the people who would soon be pouring into church, all hoping to see and kiss the body of Padre Pio.

At eight-thirty, when everything was in order, both inside and outside the church, the large bronze doors were opened. The crowd entered and hurried towards the body. Wailing, bitter weeping, and heart-rending cries filled the Church of Santa Maria delle Grazie.

Padre Pio, now motionless, was being venerated by the crowd. Among the countless people there were scientists, important citizens and religious individuals, too numerous to mention by name.

On the evening of the 23rd, the priests thought of closing the church in order to give the Carabinieri and the Police a rest, but this proved impossible. The shouting crowd in the square pressed forward, making it necessary to reopen the doors. During the interval, the priests succeeded only in taking the casket into the sacristy, where the remains of Padre Pio were taken from the wooden casket and solemnly transposed to the metal casket in anticipation of his burial in the crypt.

By six in the evening it became a glorious spectacle. The crowd was endless, and filled the entire area of Santa Maria delle Grazie. It was a torrent of men, women, young people, children, rich and poor alike. It was difficult to direct them step-by-step through the corridor that led to the interior of the church. Film crews and photographers were in action, capturing this immense and endless mass of people, constantly replenished by new arrivals. The Public Security agents replaced the exhausted Carabinieri in their difficult duty. Padre Pio's body was placed on a higher catafalque, slightly tilted towards the crowd. A glass cover was placed over the coffin so that the body could be clearly seen. Everyone approached to kiss the coffin, while they cried, prayed, and affectionately said goodbye to the deceased Padre.

The Carabinieri and the Public Security agents constantly relieved one another as the heartfelt mourning of the Padre continued. It was very touching and surprising to see so much enthusiasm, so much faith aroused by the august Padre Pio.

On the 26th, around noon, a reluctant halt was called to the interminable crowd. The centre portals of the church were closed and only a select few remained within: some friars, Padre Pio's relatives, and the Mayor.

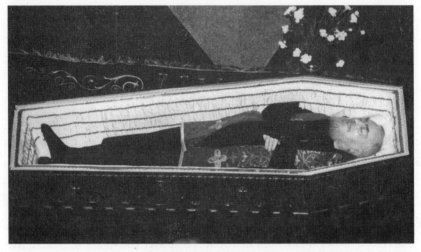

In the heart of the night
Padre Pio died at 2.30 a.m. on 23 September 1968.
His body lay in state in the church for four days so as to
receive the devoted homage of thousands of pilgrims.

At three-thirty in the afternoon, the church doors opened again and the funeral cortège marched from the church towards the village, preceded by a cordon of soldiers with drums. At 3:42 p.m., the coffin came out escorted by Carabinieri in dress uniform and platoons of Carabinieri in service uniforms. The crowd applauded. It was the last applause for this marvellous friar's virtue and stigmata. It was an applause that resounded 'Thank you!'

The cortège consisted of priests, clergy members, Capuchins with their Minister General and Minister Provincial, representatives of the government, friends, and more than one hundred thousand people who had come from all over the world. To the rear of the cortège there was another cordon of Carabinieri and Public Security agents.

A squadron of military planes hovered above the cortège, and police helicopters threw flowers and leaflets out onto the crowd.

Padre Pio, who for fifty years had remained enclosed in the Capuchin friary, was now going about the city streets, greeting the people, greeting his parents and other beloved persons who had preceded him in the cemetery.

Flowers rained down from the highly-decorated balconies, and from a microphone there came the convincing and persuasive voice of the great and illustrious scientist Prof. Enrico Medi, who was commenting on the mysteries of the rosary with touching sublimity and devoted references to the deceased Padre.

Everything took place in a calm and orderly manner, thanks to efficient plans of the Police Force, consisting of about one thousand men with their respective officers. All proceeded without incident, no harm befalling any person or thing.

The funeral was the greatest manifestation of glory, and the real triumph of Padre Pio. At seven p.m., the solemn concelebrated Mass began with the Minister General, Clementino of Vlissingen, as the main celebrant, assisted by the Bishops of Foggia and Lucera. The eulogy was given by

Fr Clemente of Santa Maria in Punta, Apostolic Administrator of the Capuchin Province of Foggia. Following other speeches, absolution was given by Bishop Antonio Cunial, Apostolic Administrator of Manfredonia. At the end, a telegram with a message from Pope Paul VI was read out: 'The august Pontiff has heard with fatherly sorrow of the pious passing of Padre Pio of Pietrelcina, and he prays the Lord to grant His faithful servant an eternal crown of justice. The Holy Father sends his apostolic blessing and condolences to the religious community in their sorrow, to the doctors, staff and patients of the Home for the Relief of Suffering, and to the entire population of San Giovanni Rotondo. Cardinal Cicognani.'

Fr Alessandro of Ripabotton wrote that, with the approval of the proper authorities, 'the ceremonies were discharged according to protocol'. At the top of the steel lid of the coffin there was a bronze and steel crucifix; at the bottom was written:

FRANCESCO FORGIONE
BORN IN PIETRELCINA 1887–5–25
DIED IN SAN GIOVANNI ROTONDO 1968–9–23

The coffin was carried to the crypt by pallbearers and placed in the locus which had been previously prepared. This took place at ten p. m., 26 September 1968.

The following day the enclosure was completed with rose-coloured steps and a sarcophagus made of a monolithic block of blue granite from Labrador, weighing over three tons.

His desire, which he expressed to the city official, Francesco Morcaldi, back in 1923, became a reality.

'I will always remember these generous people in my prayers, imploring peace and prosperity for them. As a sign of my predilection, since I am unable to do anything else, I express the desire to be buried in a quiet little corner of this land, provided that my Superiors are not opposed to it.'

'After so much upheaval,' wrote Fr Fernando of Riese Pio X, 'here will rest the exhausted remains of a man who ardently loved God and his brothers, who gave his blood for them.

'After eighty-one years of life, sixty-five of which were spent as a Capuchin, after fifty-eight years in the priesthood, during which time he unreservedly gave all – after spilling his blood for fifty years as a stigmatist – his burial in the crypt seemed to sum up his long earthly mission: *The Mass is ended.*'

The Dawn of Glorification

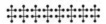

Now that the mortal life of Padre Pio is over, his body rests in a 'quiet little corner' miraculously chosen to relieve our loneliness, to testify to his sacrifice, to give evidence for his apotheosis.

His fellow priests decided that nothing short of a crypt would be a worthy grave; thus Padre Pio could remain, now and forever, in the very friary and church in which they had seen him work, in which they still see him work, and in which they will continue to see him work. A huge light shines brightly in this crypt; a bit of Paradise has descended into it.

In that tomb lies the body of a man who imitated Jesus in pain and suffering as no one else did.

In an era when the world was conquering the moon, Christ was conquering the earth. When a civilisation steeped in technology and materialism clamoured to be heard, Padre Pio replied with his God-filled silence and his immolation in the confessional. His silent testimony was so effectual that it dealt a powerful blow to those whose apostolate was materialism and agitation, and organisations which devalued spiritual life, prayer, humility, obedience, and sacrifice.

The proof that only a saint can leave such a lasting impression lies in the fact that, in spite of all their celebrity, the others are soon forgotten once they die.

One day, Padre Pio said jokingly, 'After my death there will be more hubbub than there is now.' Indeed, Padre Pio was truly a man who shook the world.

'In the light of this ideal,' wrote the Jesuit, Fr Domenico Mondrone, 'the image of Padre Pio breaks out of the restricting frame of San Giovanni Rotondo and is offered for the guidance and admiration of the entire world.

'Padre Pio is still here waiting for you, watching over each of you, listening to you, and loving you. His love has not decreased with his death; it has, instead, increased immeasurably. I am sure that not a single one of you will leave that tomb without a gift from his inexhaustible paternal love.'

From that cold, massive granite that covers his body springs forth sparks of paternal love, which each person receives in the same manner and intensity as when he was alive. This exchange of love scintillates from his body which has been rendered motionless by the laws of nature, yet effective by Divine Power.

Everyone who goes down to the crypt and kneels in front of the tomb feels that something under that massive granite is still moving, still acting. This is why an extraordinary influx of pilgrims continues without interruption, increasing with every passing day. Like a mysterious force, everyone who goes down kneels, prays, cries, and asks with the assurance of receiving.

'Padre Pio,' wrote Fr Fernando, 'during his fifty years as a stigmatist, attracted the attention of the entire world, including non-believers, to himself and his work. This attention did not cease after his death. Only the controversies ceased and were transformed to veneration.

'The greatest trial to which Padre Pio was subjected in life was excessive publicity which nearly made him more of a martyr than a confessor. The greatest proof of his virtue, now that he is dead, will come from the people as they remember his life, make pilgrimages to his tomb and ask for his esteemed and efficacious intercession.

'As in life, so in death – it is still the people, those who are truly Christian rather than those who deal in fantasies, who cling to the stigmatised Capuchin, exalting him as a man of God, as an intercessor with God.'

Considering all the good he did, and all the sacrifices he made for other people, Padre Pio should be regarded as a man full of glory.

'His glorification,' wrote Raffaele Pellecchia, Bishop of Castellammare di Stabia, '[will be the clearest reply that the Church Council] will give to this modern era; because the glory and the hope, the sorrow and agony of modern man, especially the poor and the suffering, were also the joy and hope, the sorrow and agony of Padre Pio. There was nothing genuinely human that did not echo in his heart.'

Mgr Adolfo Tortolo, Archbishop of Paraná, Argentina, believed that Padre Pio's extraordinary holiness had stirred the world, and would continue to stir it. The illustrious prelate declared that the task of putting the marvellous pages of history before mankind had just begun, a history that would tell of his divine deeds – a new 'gift', a new 'grace' that God would give mankind.

'The dawn of the glorification of Padre Pio is already here,' says the Postulator General of the Capuchin Order, Fr Bernadino of Siena.

Inquiries were made to the Sacred Congregation for the Cause of Saints regarding the disposition of the authorities in regard to opening Padre Pio's cause. A favourable reply was received and forwarded to the Minister General of the Order and his council on 31 October 1969, describing it as a 'special cause involving universal reverberations'.

Having received 'nothing to the contrary' from the Guardians of the Order, the Postulator forwarded the official request to the Bishop of Manfredonia on 4 November 1969, stating that 'Padre Pio's reputation of holiness is becoming even better known since his death.' He believed 'that such a reputation of holiness was not due to human artifice, but to the saintliness of Padre Pio's life'.

On 25 October 1971, the Archbishop of Manfredonia, Mgr Valentino Vailati, ordered the clerics and all the faithful to send all their written reports to the Holy See as soon as possible, because the preliminaries for the cause for the beatification and canonisation of Padre Pio had begun.

By the end of 1971, the Postulator General was able to say that the cause had truly made remarkable progress.

After the collection of testimonies, the preparation of a critical biography, the revision of Padre Pio's writings by two theologians, and the preparation of all the other documents – which are quite a few – the Archbishop of Manfredonia gave all the requested documentation necessary to the Sacred Congregation for the Cause of Saints on 6 January 1973. This was key in obtaining the *nihil obstat* for the introduction of the cause for the beatification and canonisation of the Servant of God, Padre Pio of Pietrelcina.

This is the work and the will of man; the remainder is being done by God through his faithful servant who is keeping his promise: 'After I die, I will do so much more.'

Afterword

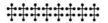

'My real mission will begin after my death.' These words that Padre Pio spoke regularly became a prophecy. Devotion to the stigmatised Padre only increased in the years after his death, as people around the world invoked him in their prayers. Today, he is one of the most invoked religious figures in Catholicism.

To those that knew him, and the many that knew of him, Padre Pio was a saint in all but name. The road to canonisation began in 1982, when the Archbishop of Manfredonia, Mgr Valentino Vailati, was authorised by the Holy See to open up the investigation into whether or not Padre Pio should be considered a saint. Of course, to so many people it was not a matter of if, but a matter of when.

Back in 1947, a young Polish priest, Fr Karol Wojtyla, was studying in Rome when he had the chance to visit Padre Pio. He spent the week in San Giovanni Rotondo attending the Padre's Masses, and later received confession from the friar.

According to Stefano Campinella, the author of several books on Padre Pio, it was then that the friar entrusted the priest with a secret – he had another wound, one that he revealed to no one else. 'It is my shoulder wound,' he told him, 'which no one knows about and has never been cured or treated.' This wound, henceforth unknown, can be equated to that which Jesus sustained as He climbed Mount Calvary. His most painful wound, as He revealed to St Bernard of Clairvaux in a vision, came not from the nails of the cross, but the heavy cross itself as He bore it on His shoulder.

It is also long rumoured – although Wojtyla denied it on many occasions – that Padre Pio had then predicted that the young priest would ascend to the highest position in the Church.

It was this priest who, years later, forged the path to Padre Pio's canonisation. Only now, the world knew him as Pope John Paul II.

The first true step to sainthood came in 1990, when Padre Pio was declared a Servant of God. From then, the Congregation for the Causes of Saints debated over the way Padre Pio lived his life, his saintliness, and all that had been said of him; the controversies and the rumours, the miracles and the intercessions.

In 1997, Pope John Paul II declared him venerable. Now the Congregation had to turn to discussing the impact Padre Pio's life had had on others, taking into account any reported miracles at his intercession. Many cases were considered, such as those already outlined in this book. In their deliberations, they took into account all his virtues, and his ability to do good, even after his death.

After two years of debating, they had come to their conclusion. In 1999, Padre Pio was declared blessed.

Two scientifically unexplained healings were approved as miracles by the Congregation: one in December 1998, that of Mrs Consiglia De Martino of Salerno, and one in December 2000, that of seven-year-old Matteo Collela, of San Giovanni Rotondo. Both were cured by Padre Pio's intercession years after his death.

On 16 June 2002, Pope John Paul II declared Padre Pio a saint, fifty-five years after the Padre had heard his confession. An estimated 300,000 people attended the canonisation ceremony, pilgrims flocking to the Vatican from all over the world.

Certainly, in the years since his death, Padre Pio has become one of the world's most famous and loved saints. Indeed, a 2006 survey by the Italian magazine *Famiglia Cristiana* found that more Italians pray to Padre Pio than to any other figure. His feast day is 23 September, the anniversary of his death, and he has been declared the patron saint of adolescents, civil defence volunteers, Pietrelcina and stress relief. His famous words 'Pray, hope, and don't worry,' have inspired many, as have his prayers, teachings, and great faith. There are now more than 3,000 'Padre Pio Prayer Groups' around the world, boasting over three million members. Parishes and shrines dedicated to the stigmatised friar can be found all across the globe.

San Giovanni Rotondo has become a centre of faith and devotion to the friar, attracting over eight million pilgrims each year. In 1995, construction of the Padre Pio Pilgrimage Church began. Designed by the renowned Italian architect Renzo Piano, the church is made of stone and glass, and can hold congregations of 6,000 people. In 2004, after much dedication and patient work, the church finally opened to the public, and Pope John Paul II himself was there to dedicate the Padre Pio Pilgrimage Church to the memory of Padre Pio.

To mark the fortieth anniversary of his death, his body was exhumed on 3 March 2008 and prepared for display in the crypt of the friary. Much of his body was in near perfect condition, and one priest remarked that he looked as though he had a manicure. His face, however, had not fared as well, and was instead coated with a silicon mask to preserve his likeness. His body was then laid out in a sepulchre of crystal, marble and silver.

On 24 April 2008, Cardinal José Saraiva Martins (then prefect of the Congregation for the Causes of the Saints) celebrated Mass in the Sanctuary of Santa Maria delle Grazie in San Giovanni Rotondo. 15,000 people arrived for this celebration of the life of Padre Pio.

Within a week, over 800,000 pilgrims made reservations to view the body of the saint. The exhibition was to last until December 2008, but only 7,200 people were able to view the crystal coffin in a day, causing them to extend it to September 2009.

Today, visitors can see Padre Pio in repose in a golden crypt in the Padre Pio Pilgrimage Church, dressed in his brown Capuchin habit with a white silk stole embroidered with crystals and golden thread. In his hands he holds a large wooden cross, a symbol of not only his devotion to God but also the stigmata by which he was known. Here he serenely rests, but the message he spread in life continues to enrapture the world. Padre Pio, the living saint, will forever more be St Pio of Pietrelcina.